MATH TRAILBLAZERS™

GRADE 3

SECOND EDITION

Student Guide

A Mathematical Journey Using Science and Language Arts

KENDALL/HUNT PUBLISHING COMPANY
4050 Westmark Drive   Dubuque, Iowa 52002

A TIMS® Curriculum
University of Illinois at Chicago

MATH TRAILBLAZERS™

Dedication

This book is dedicated to
the children and teachers
who let us see the magic
in their classrooms
and to our families who
wholeheartedly
supported us while we
searched for
ways to make it happen.

The TIMS Project

 UIC The University of Illinois
at Chicago

The original edition was based on work supported by the National Science Foundation under grant No. MDR 9050226 and the University of Illinois at Chicago. Any opinions, findings, and conclusions or recommendations expressed in this publication are those of the authors and do not necessarily reflect the views of the granting agencies.

Cover photo by Design Photography

Acknowledgments

Teaching Integrated Mathematics and Science (TIMS) Project Directors

Philip Wagreich, Principal Investigator
Joan L. Bieler
Marty Gartzman
Howard Goldberg (emeritus)
Catherine Randall Kelso

Director, Second Edition

Catherine Randall Kelso

Curriculum Developers, Second Edition

Lindy M. Chambers-Boucher
Elizabeth Colligan
Marty Gartzman
Carol Inzerillo
Catherine Randall Kelso

Jennifer Mundt Leimberer
Georganne E. Marsh
Leona Peters
Philip Wagreich

Editorial and Production Staff, Second Edition

Kathleen R. Anderson
Ai-Ai C. Cojuangco
Andrada Costoiu
Erika Larson

Cosmina Menghes
Georganne E. Marsh
Anne Roby

TIMS Professional Developers

Barbara Crum
Craig Cleve
Elizabeth Colligan
Pamela Guyton

Carol Inzerillo
Linda Miceli
Leona Peters
Jane Schlichting

TIMS Director of Media Services

Henrique Cirne-Lima

TIMS Research Staff

Catherine Randall Kelso
Barry Booton
Dibyen Majumdar

TIMS Administrative Staff

Ora Benton
David Cirillo
Enrique Puente

Acknowledgments

Principal Investigators, First Edition

Philip Wagreich, Project Director
Howard Goldberg

Senior Curriculum Developers, First Edition

Joan L. Bieler
Janet Simpson Beissinger
Astrida Cirulis
Marty Gartzman
Howard Goldberg

Carol Inzerillo
Andy Isaacs
Catherine Randall Kelso
Leona Peters
Philip Wagreich

Curriculum Developers, First Edition

Janice C. Banasiak
Lynne Beauprez
Andy Carter
Lindy M. Chambers-Boucher
Kathryn Chval
Diane Czerwinski

Jenny Knight
Sandy Niemiera
Janice Ozima
Polly Tangora
Paul Trafton

Illustrator, First Edition

Kris Dresen

Research Consultant, First Edition

Andy Isaacs

Mathematics Education Consultant, First Edition

Paul Trafton

National Advisory Committee, First Edition

Carl Berger
Tom Berger
Hugh Burkhardt
Donald Chambers
Naomi Fisher
Glenda Lappan

Mary Lindquist
Eugene Maier
Lourdes Monteagudo
Elizabeth Phillips
Thomas Post

Table of Contents

Additional student pages may be found in the
Discovery Assignment Book, the *Adventure Book*,
or the *Unit Resource Guide*.

Table of Contents

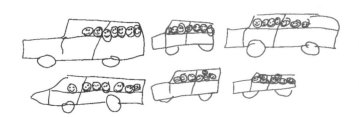

Additional student pages may be found in the *Discovery Assignment Book*, the *Adventure Book*, or the *Unit Resource Guide*.

Table of Contents

Additional student pages may be found in the *Discovery Assignment Book*, the *Adventure Book*, or the *Unit Resource Guide*.

Table of Contents

Additional student pages may be found in the *Discovery Assignment Book,* the *Adventure Book,* or the *Unit Resource Guide.*

Letter to Parents

Dear Parents,

Math Trailblazers™ is based on the ideas that mathematics is best learned through solving many different kinds of problems and that all children deserve a challenging mathematics curriculum. The program provides a careful balance of concepts and skills. Traditional arithmetic skills and procedures are covered through their repeated use in problems and through distributed practice. *Math Trailblazers,* however, offers much more. Students using this program will become proficient problem solvers, will know when and how to apply the mathematics they have learned, and will be able to clearly communicate their mathematical knowledge. Computation, measurement, geometry, data collection and analysis, estimation, graphing, patterns and relationships, mental arithmetic, and simple algebraic ideas are all an integral part of the curriculum. They will see connections between the mathematics learned in school and the mathematics used in everyday life. And, they will enjoy and value the work they do in mathematics.

The *Student Guide* is only one component of *Math Trailblazers.* Additional material and lessons are contained in the *Discovery Assignment Book,* the *Adventure Book,* and in the teacher's *Unit Resource Guides.* If you have questions about the program, we encourage you to speak with your child's teacher.

This curriculum was built around national recommendations for improving mathematics instruction in American schools and the research that supported those recommendations. The first edition was extensively tested with thousands of children in dozens of classrooms over five years of development. In preparing this second edition, we have benefited from the comments and suggestions of hundreds of teachers and children who have used the curriculum. *Math Trailblazers* reflects our view of a complete and well-balanced mathematics program that will prepare children for the 21st century—a world in which mathematical skills will be important in most occupations and mathematical reasoning will be essential for acting as an informed citizen in a democratic society. We hope that you enjoy this exciting approach to learning mathematics and that you watch your child's mathematical abilities grow throughout the year.

Philip Wagreich

Philip Wagreich
Professor, Department of Mathematics, Statistics, and Computer Science
Director, Institute for Mathematics and Science Education
The *Math Trailblazers* Team
Teaching Integrated Mathematics and Science (TIMS) Project
University of Illinois at Chicago

Unit  1

SAMPLING AND CLASSIFYING

	Student Guide	Discovery Assignment Book	Adventure Book	Unit Resource Guide*
Lesson 1				
First Names	◎	◎		◎
Lesson 2				
Turn Over	◎			
Lesson 3				
Kind of Bean	◎	◎		◎
Lesson 4				
Line Math Puzzles		◎		
Lesson 5				
You Can't Do That			◎	
Lesson 6				
A Sample of Problems	◎			

Unit Resource Guide pages are from the teacher materials.

First Names

Elizabeth and Pascal like to play computer games. One day, while playing Math-o-Rama, they tried to type their first names, but the game only let them type five letters.

> Hey! My name has six letters in it. P-a-s-c-a-l.

> And mine is spelled E-l-i-z-a-b-e-t-h! Why can't we type our full names?

What number of letters should players be able to type for their names? Elizabeth and Pascal asked their classmates to help them find out. First, students wrote their first names on small slips of paper. Then, they wrote the number of letters in their names.

They put the information in a data table. Here is the data that Elizabeth and Pascal recorded for their class.

L Number of Letters in First Name	Names of Students
1	
2	
3	
4	Dana L=4, Seth L=4, Katy L=4, Ivan L=4, Eric L=4
5	Jason L=5, Jason L=5, Jamie L=5, Peter L=5, Colin L=5, Aesis L=5, Brian L=5
6	Joseph L=6, Andrew L=6, Jordan L=6, Merley L=6, Darius L=6, Amanda L=6, Miguel L=6, Samuel L=6
7	Zachary L=7, Kristin L=7, Anthony L=7, Melissa L=7, Kenneth L=7, Kathryn L=7, Jeffrey L=7, Melissa L=7, Nicolas L=7, Natasha L=7
8	
9	Elizabeth L=9
10	
11	Christopher L=11

Elizabeth and Pascal made a graph of their data.

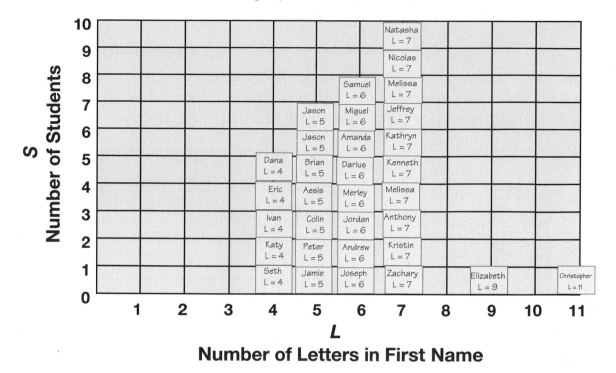

Number of Letters in First Name

"Can you see a pattern?" asked Pascal. "Yes," said Elizabeth. "No one has a first name with one, two, or three letters." "That's right!" said Pascal. "And only two kids have more than seven letters in their first name."

We will carry out an investigation called *First Names*. You will be collecting data with your class and graphing it. First, you will find the number of letters in your classmates' first names. Then, you will look for patterns in the data. Later, you will use the information to write a letter to a game company about the number of letters that a computer game should allow for a player's name.

What first names will your class use? Some children in your class might use shortened names for first names, like "Bob" for "Robert." Others might have two-part names, like "Mary Pat." Some children might even use nicknames, like "Digger." Discuss and decide with your class what you mean by "first name."

Collect

Write your first name and the number of letters in your name on a slip of paper like the ones below. Discuss with your class what the variable *L* stands for. Put the class data in a table like the one below.

Jason
L = 5

Melissa
L = 7

L Number of Letters in First Name	Names of Students
1	
2	
3	
4	Dana L = 4 Seth L = 4 Katy L = 4 Ivan L = 4 Eric L = 4
5	Jason L = 5 Jason L = 5 Jamie L = 5 Peter L = 5 Colin L = 5 Aesis L = 5 Brian L = 5

Discuss with your class how you might make the table easier to read. Then copy the class data onto the data table on *First Names Data Table and Graph* Activity Page in the *Discovery Assignment Book*.

Graph

Discuss with your class how to make a class graph of your data. Decide which variable you will graph on the **horizontal axis** and which variable you will graph on the **vertical axis**.

Use the data table to make a bar graph on *First Names Data Table and Graph*.

Use your data to answer the following questions about the first names in your class.

1. How many letters are in the longest name?

2. How many letters are in the shortest name?

3. What is the most common number of letters?

4. How many students have names with six letters?

5. How many students have names with five letters?

6. Do more than half the students have names with either six or seven letters? How did you figure this out?

7. What is the shape of the graph? Why does it have this shape?

8. Compare the graph and the data table. How are they alike? How different?

are the same height? Why?

above every number on the
at does this mean?

You make predictions every day. **Predictions** are statements that you make based on what you know and the patterns you see.

You might predict snowy weather when the temperature is cold and you see big, dark clouds in the sky. You might even predict that the next jelly bean you pull from a bag will be red because you know the bag has more red jelly beans in it than any other color.

We look at patterns to see what is most **likely** to happen. Then, we make predictions based on that information.

11. Pretend a new student is coming to class. What can you predict about the length of his or her name?

12. How would the graph change if we added all the third grade classes in our school?

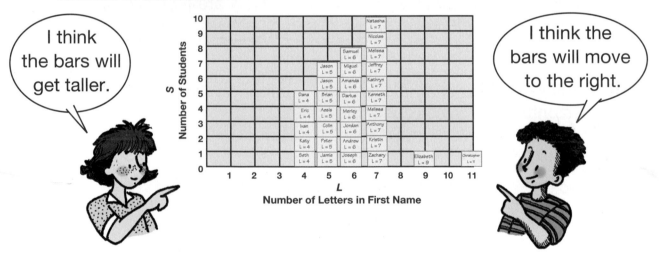

13. With your class, discuss who is right. Explain your thinking.

14. How would the graph change if everyone in class added two names from their family? Discuss with your class.

15. What number of letters should computer games allow for first names? Write a letter to the TIMS Game Company to let them know. Explain the investigation you did and the results that helped you reach your decision.

Turn Over

This is a game for two or more people. You need a deck of digit cards.

Rules:

1. Put all the cards face up.

2. Decide on a target number. Start with a small number, such as 20.

3. Each player turns over one of the digit cards on his or her turn. Keep track of the sum of all the cards turned over.

4. The player who turns over the card that makes the sum equal to or greater than the target number is the winner.

5. Play several games with the same target number. Then, select other target numbers between 20 and 35.

6. Discuss strategies for winning.

Kind of Bean

Sampling a Population

What is a population?

A **population** is a group or collection of things. The population of your city or town is the group of people who live there.

Sometimes, a population is too big to study or too hard to count. Then, you count a sample of the population. A **sample** is a smaller group or part of the whole population.

If you want to learn about the population of pets in your town, you can begin by counting the number of dogs, cats, birds, and other pets on your block.

Using the information from your block, you can predict the kinds of pets that people in your town own.

You can also use your data to predict which pet is the most common in your town or neighborhood.

Kind of Bean

A Sample of Animals

Betty Robinson and her scientist parents are studying animals in the Amazon rain forest. The population of animals in the rain forest is very large, so Betty and her parents study a sample of the animals. They have chosen a small area of the forest to investigate. They identify the types of animals they see in this area and count the number of each type of animal. The two main **variables** in their experiment are the type of animal and the number of each type.

I counted 35 spider monkeys in that troop.

They use the TIMS Laboratory Method to help them solve problems. First, they **draw a picture** of the steps they will follow in the experiment.

Then, they **collect and organize** the data in a data table.

They then **graph** their data.

Finally, they **analyze and discuss** their results.

When you have a problem, you, too, can use the tools of science to solve it. We call these tools of science the **TIMS Laboratory Method**.

T Type of Animal	N Number
Spider Monkeys	230
Squirrels	175
River Otters	75
Armadillos	200
Jaguars	50

Here is the graph of the Robinsons' data.

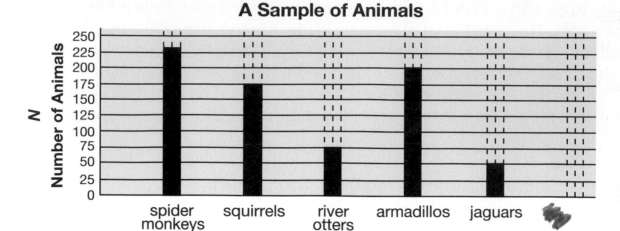

A Sample of Animals

Discuss

1. What variables do the letters *T* and *N* stand for?

2. What variable is on the horizontal axis?

3. What variable is on the vertical axis?

4. At the beginning of the experiment, the Robinsons chose **values** for the variable Type of Animal. Two of these values are spider monkeys and jaguars. What are the other values for this variable?

5. What values for the variable Number of Animals did the Robinsons record in their data table?

6. What is the most common animal in the sample?

7. What is the least common animal in the sample?

8. Predict which two animals are the most common in the whole population.

You are going to conduct an experiment called *Kind of Bean* using the TIMS Laboratory Method. You will use different kinds of beans in a container to stand for different animals in the rain forest. Your job will be to pull a sample of beans from a larger container and count the number of each kind of bean. Using the data, you will predict which kind of bean is the most common and which is the least common.

A Sample of Problems

1. Alex wants to print name cards for the four students in his group. The other members of his group are Beth, Anna, and Todd. How many letters will he print?

2. Make a list of the first names of five students from your class. How many letters are in this list?

3. Choose some first names from your class so that the total number of letters is twenty-two. Write a number sentence for this problem.

4. **A.** Four students are playing a game of Turn Over. The target number is 25. Alex turned over an eight. Stephen turned over a five. Then, Christa turned over a three. What is the sum of their cards?

   B. Now it is Maricella's turn. What card does she need to turn over to win the game?

5. Kathy, Biruté, Jay, and Joanie were playing Turn Over. They each turned over one card. The sum of their cards was 26. Kathy turned over a 5. Biruté turned over an 8. What could Jay and Joanie have turned over?

6. Professor Peabody took a sample of sixteen beans from a container. He recorded two lima beans and nine pinto beans. He forgot to record the number of navy beans before he dumped them back into the container. How many navy beans were in his sample?

7. In Rachel's sample there were fifteen pinto beans, four lima beans, and seven navy beans. Sheila said, "I pulled the same number of navy beans as you. I have two more pinto beans than you. I have one less lima bean than you." How many beans did Sheila pull?

8. Betty Robinson and her parents collected data on a small sample of animals. They saw 22 spider monkeys, 18 squirrels, 9 river otters, 20 armadillos, and 5 jaguars. About how many animals are in the sample?

Unit 2
STRATEGIES: An Assessment Unit

	Student Guide	Discovery Assignment Book	Adventure Book	Unit Resource Guide*
Lesson 1				
Addition Facts Strategies	◎	◎		◎
Lesson 2				
Spinning Sums	◎	◎		
Lesson 3				
Yü the Great A Chinese Legend			◎	
Lesson 4				
Magic Squares	◎	◎		
Lesson 5				
Subtraction Facts Strategies	◎	◎		
Lesson 6				
Spinning Differences		◎		◎
Lesson 7				
Assessing the Subtraction Facts		◎		
Lesson 8				
Number Sense with Dollars and Cents	◎			

Unit Resource Guide pages are from the teacher materials.

Addition Facts Strategies

What strategies can you use to solve 6 + 10 + 4?

"There are many different ways to solve addition problems," said Miriam.

"I can think of at least two ways," said Eric. "You can count up using your fingers and toes or you can use blocks or cubes."

"I like to find groups of ten, then add up what's left over," said Miriam.

Miriam and Eric used counters to help Tisha and Peter solve 6 + 10 + 4.

You can put together the four and six to make a ten.

Switching

Do the following problems in your head. Make as many groups of ten as possible. There may be more than one way to solve each problem. A sample has been done for you.

Sample Problem: 4 + 9 + 6 =

Make a ten with the 4 and 6. Then, add the 9. The answer is 19.

1. 5 + 6 + 5 =

2. 12 + 7 + 8 =

3. 5 + 9 + 11 =

4. 3 + 17 + 7 =

5. 16 + 4 + 11 =

6. 14 + 16 + 6 =

Breaking Addends into Parts

Find groups of ten in the following number sentences by breaking an addend into two parts. Then, find the sum. There may be more than one way to solve each problem. Be ready to explain your thinking to the class.

Sample Problem: 5 + 9 + 6 =

Break the 9 into 5 + 4.
Find a group of 10.
See if there are more tens.
Find the sum.

$(5 + 5) + (4 + 6) =$
$10 + 10 = 20$

7. 16 + 6 + 2 =

8. 5 + 12 + 7 =

9. 14 + 8 + 1 =

10. 13 + 2 + 9 =

11. 14 + 12 + 4 =

12. 22 + 16 + 5 =

Spinning Sums

Lisa, Douglas, and Carla were playing a board game using spinners. Lisa went first. She spun a 5 and a 4, so she got to move 9 spaces on the board. The **sum** of 5 and 4 is 9.

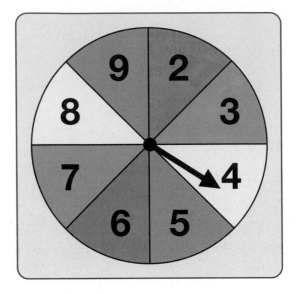

Douglas spun a 3 and an 8, so he got to move 11 spaces on the board. Carla got to move 7 spaces.

Discuss the following questions with your class.

1. What numbers could Carla have spun to move seven spaces?

2. What is the largest sum a player can spin?

3. Which do you think is more likely to happen: spinning a sum of 7 or spinning a sum of 18?

The Most Common Sum

Lisa, Douglas, and Carla wanted to know what sum they could expect to spin most often. They decided to spin both spinners 40 times. They wrote down the number sentences in a data table. Then, they made a graph.

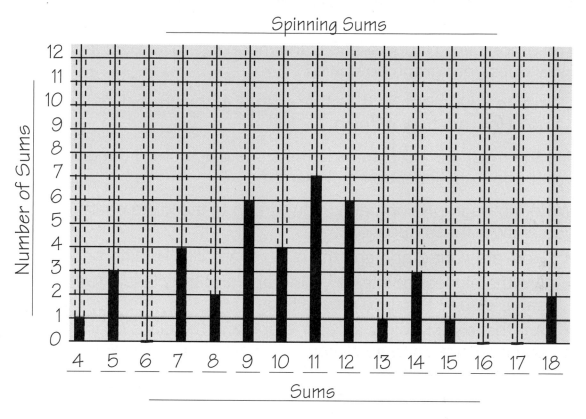

Spinning Sums

Spin two spinners 40 times. Write down a number sentence and sum for each spin on the *Spinning Sums Data Table.* Use your data to make a graph.

Discuss the following questions with your class. Use the data from *your* graph to answer the questions.

4. What was *your* most common sum? Tell how you know.

5. What is *your* least common sum? Tell how you know.

6. Where are the tallest bars on your graph? What does it mean when the bars are tall?

7. Where are the shortest bars on your graph? What does it mean when the bars are short?

8. The graph Lisa, Douglas, and Carla made has taller bars in the middle. How does your graph compare?

9. Compare your graph to the other graphs in the class. How are they the same? How are they different?

10. Are the most common sums in the same place on all the graphs? What about the least common sums?

11. Write a paragraph comparing your graph to the class chart. Make sure you answer these questions:
    - How are your graph and the class chart alike or different?
    - Are the highest points on your graph and the class chart in the same place? What do they tell you?
    - Are the lowest points on your graph and the class chart in the same place? What do they tell you?

As a class, make a chart with all of the possible spins and sums.

Magic Squares

Magic squares are puzzles that are thousands of years old. This is a magic square.

8	9	4
3	7	11
10	5	6

1. **A.** Find the sum of each row and column.

   B. The main diagonals go from 10 to 4 and from 8 to 6. Find the sum of each main diagonal.

   C. What is special about this square?

2. Magic squares do not always have three rows and three columns. However, the number of rows is always the same as the number of columns. In the last unit, you worked on some line math puzzles. How are the two kinds of puzzles alike?

3. Try to solve another magic square. Follow these directions:
   - Use a square like the one at the right.
   - Fill in each box with the digits: 3, 3, 3, 5, 5, 5, 7, 7, 7.
   - Each main diagonal, row, and column must have a sum of 15.

   Find as many solutions as you can.

4. Try another magic square using these rules:
   - Use the digits 1, 1, 1, 5, 5, 5, 9, 9, 9.
   - The sum is 15.

   Find as many solutions as you can.

5. How are the solutions to the magic squares in Questions 3 and 4 alike?

6. Here is an incomplete magic square.

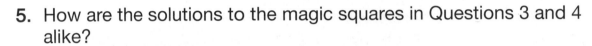

7	12	5
		10
11		

   A. What is the sum?
   B. Use the digits 4, 6, 8, and 9 to complete the magic square.

Homework

Use the digits from the *Digits* Activity Page in the *Discovery Assignment Book*.

1. Try to solve a different magic square. Use these rules:
   - Use the digits 3, 3, 3, 6, 6, 6, 9, 9, 9.
   - The sum is 18.

   Find as many solutions as you can, and write your answers on a sheet of paper. Hint: Compare this magic square to the ones you created in Questions 3 and 4 during class.

2. Here is an incomplete magic square.
   A. What is the sum?
   B. Use the digits 7, 8, 9, and 11 to complete the magic square. Remember that each row, column, and main diagonal must have the same sum.

		13
14	10	6
	12	

3. Try to find another solution for a magic square with the same sum as the one in Question 2. Begin with a blank magic square, and use the digits 6, 7, 8, 9, 10, 11, 12, 13, 14.

4. Here is another incomplete magic square.
   A. What is the sum?
   B. Use the digits 7, 9, 10, 12, 13, and 15 to fill in the blanks.

		8
	11	
14		

Subtraction Facts Strategies

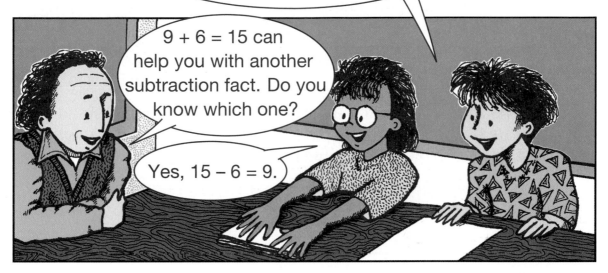

1. What strategies can you use to solve 16 – 9?

2. What strategies can you use to solve 16 – 7?

3. What strategies can you use to solve 18 – 10?

4. Anna used addition to help her find the answer to a subtraction fact. She said, "5 + 9 = 14." What subtraction fact or facts can she solve using this addition fact?

5. Roberto is trying to find the answer to 15 – 6. He counts up and says, "from 6 to 10 is 4 and from 10 to 15 is 5." Explain how he might use these numbers to help him solve the fact 15 – 6.

6. Sam said, "I know 5 – 2 = 3. I don't use any strategy for that fact. I just know it!" Name three subtraction facts you just know.

Nine, Ten

To play this game, you need:
- *Spinners 11–18 and 9–10*
- 2 clear plastic spinners or 2 pencils with paper clips
- 2 game boards

The first person to fill in one of the columns on his or her game board is the winner.

1. Make two game boards, one for each player, like the one below.

Subtract 9	Subtract 10

First Spin

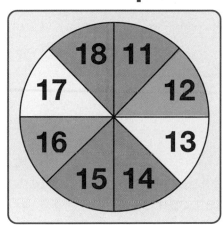

Second Spin

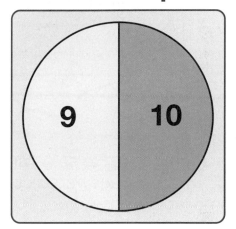

2. Place the plastic spinners over the *Spinners 11–18 and 9–10.* If you do not have clear spinners, use pencils and paper clips. Your teacher will show you how.

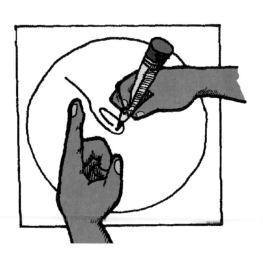

3. Spin both spinners. On the first spinner, you will spin a number from 11 to 18. On the second spinner, you will spin either a 9 or a 10.

4. Make a subtraction sentence with the two numbers you spin. If your partner agrees that your answer is correct, write the number sentence in the game board column where it belongs. If it is not correct, you do not write anything on the game board.

5. Take turns with your partner until one of you has completely filled in one column.

Suzanne and John's Game

Suzanne and John are playing *Nine, Ten.* Suzanne spins an 11 and a 9, so she says, "11 minus 9 equals 2." Since she answered correctly, she writes the number sentence in the column labeled "Subtract 9" on her game board.

Subtract 9	Subtract 10
$11 - 9 = 2$	

Now, it's John's turn. He spins an 18 and a 10, so he says, "18 minus 10 equals 8." Since he answered correctly, he writes the number sentence in the column labeled "Subtract 10" on his game board.

Subtract 9	Subtract 10
	$18 - 10 = 8$

After playing a while longer, the game boards looked like this:

Suzanne's Board

Subtract 9	Subtract 10
11 − 9 = 2	17 − 10 = 7
17 − 9 = 8	15 − 10 = 5
15 − 9 = 6	11 − 10 = 1
18 − 9 = 9	

John's Board

Subtract 9	Subtract 10
18 − 9 = 9	18 − 10 = 8
13 − 9 = 4	12 − 10 = 2
18 − 9 = 9	13 − 10 = 3
	16 − 10 = 6
	16 − 10 = 6

Notice that John recorded 16 − 10 = 6 twice. He spun the same numbers on two different turns. He answered the problem correctly both times. John won the game because he completely filled in one column first.

Play a game with a friend. Look for patterns in the number sentences on the game boards when you finish playing.

Number Sense with Dollars and Cents

Number Sense with Dollars and Cents

Solve the following problems in your head. Explain your thinking. The prices are listed on the picture of the fruit stand at the farmer's market.

1. A. How many cents are in one quarter?
   B. How many cents are in two quarters?
   C. How many cents are in three quarters?

2. A. How many quarters are in $1.00?
   B. How many quarters are in $1.50?
   C. How many quarters are in $2.50?
   D. How many quarters are in $4.00?

3. Pretend you are going to the farmer's market with quarters.
   A. Do you need two or three quarters to buy a bunch of grapes?
   B. How many quarters do you need to buy one plum?

4. Joel has $1.00 to spend. Can he buy four plums?

5. Can Joel buy a bunch of grapes and one pear?

6. Joel loves apple cider. If he buys one quart of cider, what else can he buy?

7. Miguel has $1.50.
   A. How many pears can he buy?
   B. How many plums can he buy?

8. Can Miguel buy three apples and one pear?

9. If Miguel buys a quart of apple cider, what else can he buy?

10. Can Miguel buy one apricot, one apple, and one bunch of grapes?

11. If you had $2.00 to spend at the farmer's market, what would you buy?

Unit 3
Exploring Multiplication

	Student Guide	Discovery Assignment Book	Adventure Book	Unit Resource Guide*
Lesson 1				
T-Shirt Factory Problems	@			
Lesson 2				
In Twos, Threes, and More	@	@		
Lesson 3				
Multiplication Stories	@			
Lesson 4				
Making Teams		@		
Lesson 5				
Multiples on the Calendar				@
Lesson 6				
More T-Shirt Problems	@			

Unit Resource Guide pages are from the teacher materials.

T-Shirt Factory Problems

The third-grade students at Washington School are making T-shirts with their first names written on them. They plan to buy letters from a craft store and sew them onto the T-shirts. They collected data and made the graph below.

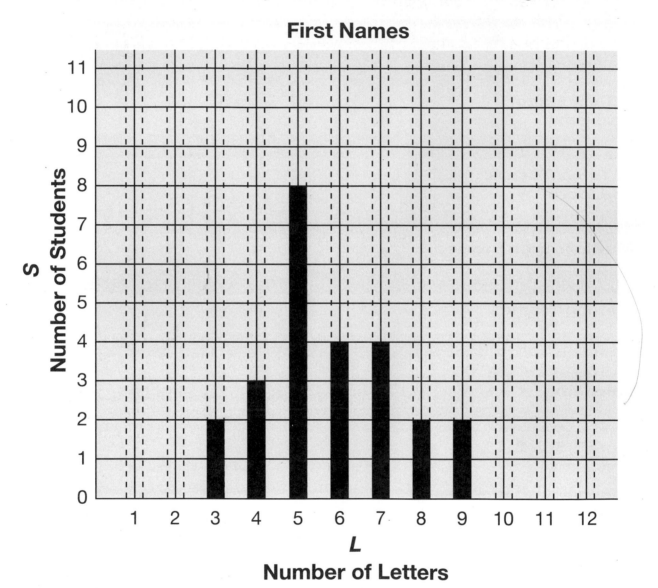

First Names

Number of Students (S) vs *Number of Letters (L)*

The students worked in groups. All the students with the same number of letters in their first names were in the same group. For example, all the students with four letters in their first names worked in one group and all the students with five letters in their first names worked in another.

Use the graph to solve the following problems. Explain how you solved each problem. Try to use a number sentence to show your thinking.

1. **A.** There are three students in the class who have four letters in their names. Their names are Levi, Mara, and John. Draw a picture of their three T-shirts with their names on them.

   B. How many letters will they have to buy altogether?

2. **A.** How many students have eight letters in their names?

   B. How many letters will these students need to buy in order to write all their names on all their T-shirts?

3. **A.** How many students have six letters in their names?

   B. How many letters will these students need to buy in order to write all their names on all their T-shirts?

4. Each letter costs 10 cents. How much will it cost to buy all the letters for the group with three letters in their names?

5. How much will it cost to buy all the letters for the group with five letters in their names?

6. **A.** Which group will need more letters, the group with five letters in their names or the group with seven letters?

   B. How many more letters will that group need?

7. How much will the letters cost for the group with nine letters?

8. How many letters are needed to make T-shirts for the whole class?

In Twos, Threes, and More

Use the picture to answer the following questions.

1. There are four clocks in the picture, and each clock has three hands. How many hands are there on all the clocks? How did you find out?

2. The clock hands come in four groups of three hands. Other things in the picture also come in groups. Some of them are listed below. How many of each item are there altogether? Explain how you found your answers.

   A. Tennis balls in packages

   B. Eyes on dolls

   C. Legs on horses

   D. Teacups in tea sets

   E. Wheels on motorcycles

3. Tina the Tennis Pro bought five packages of tennis balls.

   A. How many tennis balls did she buy altogether?

   B. Write a multiplication sentence that shows your answer.

4. Mary received two Tea Time sets for her birthday. How many people can she invite to a tea party?

5. Shelly's family has three watches. One watch has two hands. Each of the other two watches has three hands. How many hands are on the watches altogether? Explain how you got your answer.

6. Alex bought one of the horses. How many legs are on the horses in the store now?

Homework

1. **A.** How many people are in your family?

   B. How many toes does your family have altogether? Explain how you got your answer.

   C. Complete a multiplication sentence like the following that shows your answer.

   $$\underline{\hspace{3cm}} \times 10 = \underline{\hspace{2cm}}$$

2. **A.** How many chairs are at the table where you eat?

   B. How many legs are there on all the chairs at your table? Explain how you found your answer.

   C. Write a multiplication sentence that shows your answer.

   $$\underline{\hspace{3cm}} \times 4 = \underline{\hspace{2cm}}$$

3. **A.** Kim has eight stuffed animals. How many eyes do her stuffed animals have altogether? Explain how you got your answer.

   B. Write a multiplication sentence that shows your answer.

4. **A.** Joanne bought 4 six-packs of juice boxes as a treat for her soccer team. How many juice boxes did she bring?

   B. Write a multiplication sentence that shows your answer.

5. **A.** Hot dog buns come in packs of eight. How many buns are in three packs?

   B. Write a number sentence that shows your answer.

6. **A.** How many days are in 4 weeks?

   B. Write a number sentence that shows your answer.

7. **A.** Draw a picture of something that you find in your home that comes in a group.

   B. Write a multiplication sentence that describes your picture.

Multiplication Stories

In math class, students were using computers. They wrote stories and drew pictures to show how they solved some problems. They called it "story solving." As you read through these stories, you can think about what kind of pictures you would draw or what kind of stories you would write.

Their first problem was: How much is 7×5?

1. Here is the picture Jerome and Alex drew on a computer. How many clouds did they draw? How many strikes of lightning did they draw?

Here is the story Jerome and Alex wrote about 7×5:

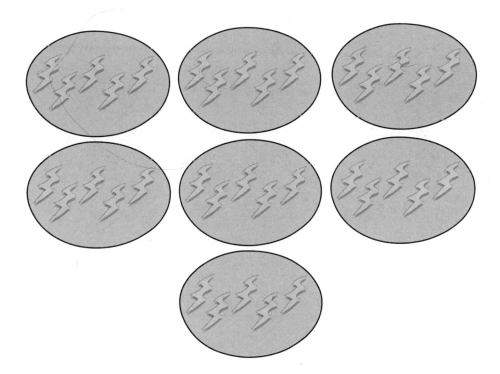

We made 7 clouds. We put 5 strikes of lightning on each one.
We found that 7 times 5 equals 35. We counted by fives 7 times.

Multiplication Stories

Natalia and Sheena made this picture to help them find the answer to 7 × 3.

This is the story Natalia and Sheena wrote:

> We made 7 circles, and we put 3 cats in each circle. We found out that
> it was 21 when we counted all of the cats by ones. 7 × 3 = 21

Robert made this picture and wrote this story:

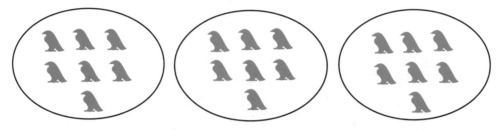

7 + 7 + 7 = 21. I put 7 birds in 3 big circles. 3 × 7 = 21. The end.

Sheena looked at both pictures. She saw that 7 × 3 = 21 and 3 × 7 = 21.
She said, "I know how they came out the same. I found seven threes."
Then, she drew seven boxes on Robert's picture like this:

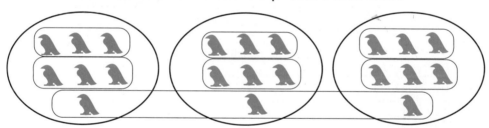

2. How did Sheena change Robert's picture? What does Sheena's
   work show?

3. Igor drew his picture using pencil and paper. He solved the problem: How much is 6 × 7? Look at Igor's picture and work. How did he solve the problem?

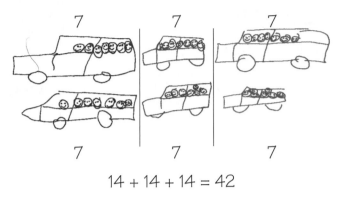

14 + 14 + 14 = 42

Igor wrote this story:

There are six cars in the park and there are seven people in each one. 6 × 7 = 42

4. Kevin and Chanel worked on this problem: How much is 4 × 20? They decided to use connecting cubes to solve the problem. They made four trains of cubes. How long is each train?

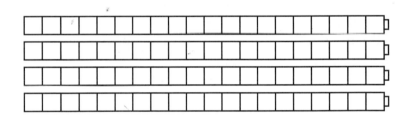

They divided each train into two trains of ten cubes so that they could count by tens.

10		50	
20		60	
30		70	
40		80	

5. Look at the picture. How much is 4 × 20?

Marta drew the following picture to answer the problem: How much is $5 \times \frac{1}{4}$?

Marta wrote: Five friends ate pizza at a sleep-over. Each girl ate $\frac{1}{4}$ pizza. They ate $1\frac{1}{4}$ pizzas.

6. What picture would you draw to answer the problem: How much is $5 \times \frac{1}{4}$?

7. Draw pictures and write your own stories to solve each problem. Write number sentences for each story.

   A. 3×4 **B.** 7×8 **C.** 9×5

   D. 7×10 **E.** $4 \times \frac{1}{2}$ **F.** $5 \times \frac{1}{2}$

Homework

Write a story and draw a picture to show how to solve each problem. Share your stories with a family member.

   I. A. 7×4 **B.** 6×10 **C.** 6×9

   2. A. $2 \times \frac{1}{2}$ **B.** 4×5 **C.** 2×30

More T-Shirt Problems

For each problem below, explain how you solved it.

1. There are 24 students in a class at Mann School. Every student in the class made a T-shirt with the name of the school written on it.

    A. How many letters did students have to buy to write "Mann School" on each T-shirt?

    B. The class divided into six groups to decorate the T-shirts. Each of these groups had the same number of students. How many children were in each group?

2. Ali took 20 minutes to sew the letters on her T-shirt. Michael took three times as long. How long did Michael take?

3. Jennifer took 40 minutes to sew on her letters. Ryan took half as long. How long did Ryan take?

4. A. How many minutes are in an hour?

    B. Victoria took 1 hour and 10 minutes to sew on her letters. Emma took 25 minutes. How much longer did Victoria take than Emma?

5. Jason decorated his T-shirt with the faces of his friends. He put four faces in five rows. How many faces are on Jason's T-shirt?

6. Rosa decorated her T-shirt with flowers. She put seven flowers in three rows.

    A. How many flowers are on her T-shirt?

    B. It took Rosa 30 minutes to sew on her first row of seven flowers. How long did it take to sew all the flowers on her T-shirt?

7. Carlita decorated her T-shirt with 20 stars. She has four rows. How many stars should she put in each row?

8. The Mann School marching band has 5 students in a row and six rows. How many students are in the band?

Unit 4
PLACE VALUE CONCEPTS

	Student Guide	Discovery Assignment Book	Adventure Book	Unit Resource Guide*
Lesson 1				
Breaking Numbers into Parts		◎		◎
Lesson 2				
The TIMS Candy Company	◎	◎		◎
Lesson 3				
Base-Ten Addition	◎	◎		
Lesson 4				
Bubble Sort				
Lesson 5				
It's Time	◎	◎		◎
Lesson 6				
Time for Problems	◎			

Unit Resource Guide pages are from the teacher materials.

The TIMS Candy Company

The TIMS Candy Company makes chocolate candies called Chocos. Their chocolate is quite popular, and people love to order it.

The TIMS Candy Company keeps track of its candy with **base-ten pieces.**

A **bit** is worth 1 Choco.

A **skinny** is worth 10 Chocos. That means it's worth the same as 10 bits.

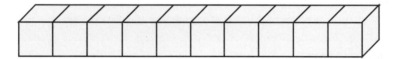

A **flat** is worth 100 Chocos. That means it's worth the same as 10 skinnies or 100 bits.

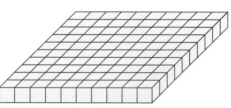

A **pack** is worth 1000 Chocos. That means it's worth the same as 10 flats, 100 skinnies, or 1000 bits.

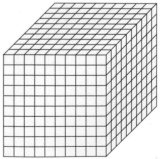

The workers at the TIMS Candy Company put their base-ten pieces on a *Base-Ten Board*. They record the number of Chocos shown in each column on the *Base-Ten Recording Sheet*.

The TIMS Candy Company

Kris made 357 Chocos. This is how he recorded his work.

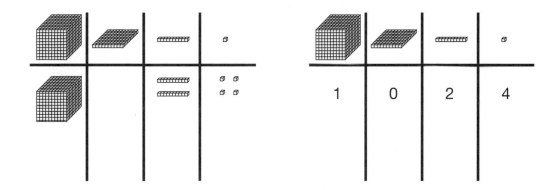

1. Kris made 3 flats of Chocos. How many Chocos is that?

2. Kris made 5 skinnies of Chocos. How many Chocos is that?

3. Kris made 7 bits of Chocos. How many Chocos is that?

4. Write the total number of Chocos Kris made in words.

Alissa's work is shown below.

5. Alissa made 1 pack of Chocos. How many Chocos is that?

6. Alissa made 2 skinnies of Chocos. How many Chocos is that?

7. Alissa made 4 bits of Chocos. How many Chocos is that?

8. Write the total number of Chocos Alissa made in words.

The TIMS Candy Company receives many orders for its Chocos.

Use your base-ten pieces to show how many Chocos were ordered for each order slip below.

9.
TIMS Candy Co.
Order Slip 1   87 Chocos

10.
TIMS Candy Co.
Order Slip 2   709 Chocos

11.
TIMS Candy Co.
Order Slip 3   1444 Chocos

12.
TIMS Candy Co.
Order Slip 4   395 Chocos

13.
TIMS Candy Co.
Order Slip 5   2010 Chocos

14.
TIMS Candy Co.
Order Slip 6   99 Chocos

15.
TIMS Candy Co.
Order Slip 7   2357 Chocos

16.
TIMS Candy Co.
Order Slip 8   1110 Chocos

17.
TIMS Candy Co.
Order Slip 9   876 Chocos

Base-Ten Shorthand

The TIMS Candy Company sometimes uses special symbols as shorthand when they don't have their base-ten pieces. They call this **base-ten shorthand.**

• = Bit | = Skinny   ▢ = Flat   ▱ = Pack

So, the shorthand for 1532 is

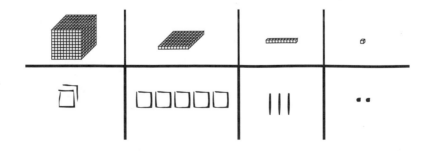

The Fewest Pieces Rule

The TIMS Candy Company uses the Fewest Pieces Rule to keep track of each order of Chocos. That means the order for 323 Chocos is shown like this:

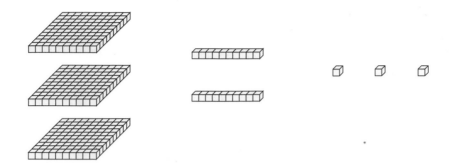

Michael, an employee at the TIMS Candy Company, is keeping track of his orders. He is learning to use the Fewest Pieces Rule without the *Base-Ten Board.* Check his work for each of the orders below. For Questions 18 through 26, answer *each* of these two questions.

   A. Did Michael use the Fewest Pieces Rule to keep track of the order? If not, use base-ten shorthand to correct his work.

   B. How much candy was ordered?

18. Michael showed an order with 1 pack, 4 skinnies, 3 flats, and 4 bits.

19. Michael showed an order with 2 packs, 7 flats, 4 skinnies, and 11 bits.

20. Michael showed an order with 1 pack, 5 flats, 16 skinnies, and 3 bits.

21. Michael showed an order with 2 packs, 12 flats, 5 skinnies, and 4 bits.

22. Michael showed an order with 8 flats, 10 skinnies, and 5 bits.

23. Michael showed an order with 5 packs, 3 skinnies, and 7 bits.

24. Michael showed an order with 7 flats, 4 packs, and 7 bits.

25. Michael showed an order with 10 flats, 14 skinnies, 2 packs, and 2 bits.

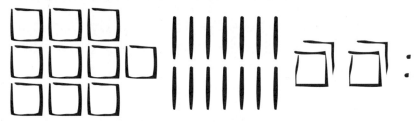

26. Michael showed an order with 3 packs, 20 skinnies, 11 flats, and 11 bits.

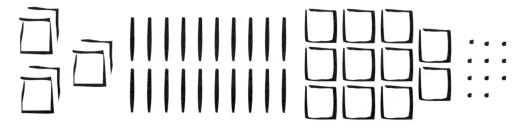

This is the number of Chocos the TIMS Candy Company made in a week.

Monday	Tuesday	Wednesday	Thursday	Friday
5789	1057	5879	592	678

27. Which day did the company produce the most Chocos?

28. Which day did the company produce the least Chocos?

29. Write the numbers in order from least to greatest.

Michelle ordered some Chocos from the TIMS Candy Company. Here is how the TIMS Candy Company used base-ten pieces to show her order.

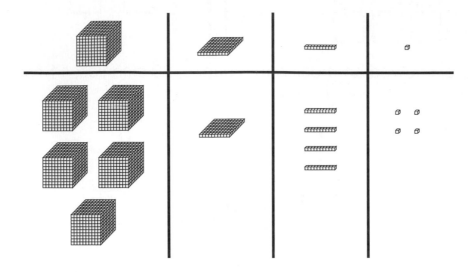

1. How many Chocos are in the packs Michelle ordered?

2. How many Chocos are in the flats Michelle ordered?

3. How many Chocos are in the skinnies Michelle ordered?

4. How many Chocos are in the bits Michelle ordered?

5. How many Chocos in all did Michelle order?

6. Write in words the total number of Chocos Michelle ordered.

7. Howard ordered 5270 Chocos. Is this more or less than the number Michelle ordered?

8. Kay ordered five thousand eighty-one Chocos. Is this more or less than the number Michelle ordered?

9. Show these numbers with base-ten shorthand.
   A. 1752
   B. 370
   C. 5034
   D. 1755

Using the Fewest Pieces Rule

10. Write the number of Chocos this worker packed. Did she use the fewest pieces possible? If not, use base-ten shorthand to show the order with the fewest pieces possible. Write in words the amount of each order.

A.

B.

C.

11. Write the following numbers in order from **smallest** to **largest**.

5765   7589   5753   589   7980

12. Write the following numbers in order from **largest** to **smallest**.

8976   789   924   9023   8724

Base-Ten Addition

Addition with Base-Ten Pieces

Andy and Alda work at the TIMS Candy Company. On Monday, Andy made 42 Chocos. Alda made 36 Chocos. They recorded their work on the *Base-Ten Board* and on the *Base-Ten Recording Sheet*.

		4	2
+		3	6
		7	8

Andy said that 2 bits and 6 bits make 8 bits and that 4 skinnies and 3 skinnies make 7 skinnies. Together, Andy and Alda made 78 Chocos. They recorded this as 7 skinnies and 8 bits above.

On Tuesday, Andy made 28 Chocos while Alda made 54. Andy said that together they made 7 skinnies and 12 bits of Chocos.

		2	8
+		5	4
		7	12

"You're not using the Fewest Pieces Rule," said Alda. Alda traded 10 bits for a skinny. Then, there were 8 skinnies and 2 bits. Together, they made 82 Chocos.

		2	8
	+	5	4
		7 ^{1}	̶1̶2̶
		8	2

1. "We don't need a record sheet or columns if we use the Fewest Pieces Rule," said Alda. Look at the two ways Alda solved the problem below. Why did Alda put a 1 above the 3 when using the shortcut?

		3	7
	+	4	7
		7 ^{1}	̶1̶4̶
		8	4

$$\begin{array}{r} {}^{1} \\ 37 \\ + 47 \\ \hline 84 \end{array}$$

2. Complete the following problems using base-ten pieces, base-ten shorthand, or Alda's shortcut method.

A. $\begin{array}{r} 25 \\ + 30 \\ \hline \end{array}$ B. $\begin{array}{r} 47 \\ + 27 \\ \hline \end{array}$ C. $\begin{array}{r} 62 \\ + 73 \\ \hline \end{array}$ D. $\begin{array}{r} 63 \\ + 59 \\ \hline \end{array}$

E. $\begin{array}{r} 72 \\ + 48 \\ \hline \end{array}$ F. $\begin{array}{r} 27 \\ + 82 \\ \hline \end{array}$ G. $\begin{array}{r} 13 \\ 35 \\ + 26 \\ \hline \end{array}$ H. $\begin{array}{r} 28 \\ 17 \\ + 26 \\ \hline \end{array}$

3. Solve Question 2E a second way and explain your method.

It's Time

Melvin is an employee at the TIMS Candy Company. A time clock, like the one shown here, records the hours he works each day. He puts a time card in the clock when he comes to work and when he leaves. The clock records the times on the card as shown.

Time Card

Melvin   McBean

 # 6 2 4 3 6 2 1 9 5

TIME IN	TIME OUT
9:30	5:38
9:31	5:46
9:22	5:30

Record the time shown on each clock face as it would be printed on the time cards at the TIMS Candy Company.

1.

2.

3.

4.

5.

6.

7.

8.

9.

10.

11.

12.

13.

14.

15.

16.

17.

18.

Time for Problems

Use your student clock to complete the following problems. Remember to use skip counting by fives.

1. The hour hand is just before the two. The minute hand is pointing to the eight. What time is it?

2. What is another way to say the time 6:45?

3. Martha left school at 3:15 P.M. It takes her 15 minutes to walk home. What time should Martha arrive at home?

4. Shelby looked at her watch. The time was 3:25 P.M. Shelby has to be home at 4:00 P.M. How much time does Shelby still have to play outside?

5. School starts in Lincolnshire at 8:30 A.M. Draw a picture of a clock with hands showing 8:30 A.M.

6. Stacy looked at her watch. How could Stacy find out how many minutes are in one hour without counting each minute mark?

7. Marcus has band practice from 3:30 P.M. to 4:15 P.M. How many minutes does Marcus have band practice?

8. Math class starts at 1:20 P.M. It lasts 50 minutes. What time does math class end?

9. Frieda's soccer team usually practices 45 minutes. Today, Frieda's coach said, "Let's practice 15 minutes longer." How long did Frieda practice today?

10. Enrique looked at his watch. The hour hand is between the two and the three. The minute hand is pointing to the five. What time is on Enrique's watch?

Unit 5
Area of Different Shapes

	Student Guide	Discovery Assignment Book	Adventure Book	Unit Resource Guide*
Lesson 1				
Measuring Area	◎	◎		
Lesson 2				
Boo the Blob		◎		
Lesson 3				
The Better "Picker Upper"	◎	◎		
Lesson 4				
The Haunted House			◎	
Lesson 5				
Joe the Goldfish				◎
Lesson 6				
Using Number Sense at the Book Sale	◎			

Unit Resource Guide pages are from the teacher materials.

Measuring Area

What is area?

Area is a measurement of size. We measure the area of a floor to find the amount of carpet needed to cover the floor. We can also use area to measure the amount of paper needed to wrap a present.

Area is the amount of surface that is needed to cover something. To measure the area of a shape, we tell the number of squares needed to cover the shape.

Professor Peabody has started to cover his living room and hall with square tiles. The living room is in the shape of an octagon. The hall is a rectangle.

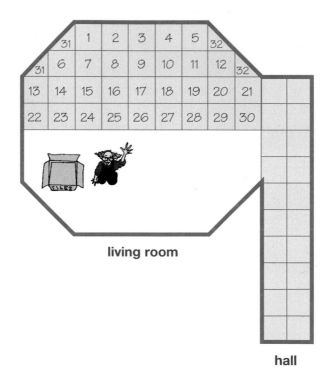

living room

hall

1. How many square tiles did Professor Peabody use to cover the hall?

2. Professor Peabody has covered half of his living room with tiles. These tiles have been counted for you. Why are the numbers 31 and 32 used twice?

3. How many square tiles will it take to cover the whole living room?

A **square centimeter** is the area of a square that is 1 centimeter long on each side. This is 1 square centimeter.

4. Find the area in square centimeters of these two shapes.

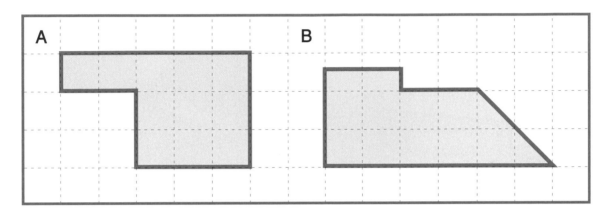

5. This shape has curved sides. Professor Peabody estimated its area by counting whole square centimeters and matching smaller pieces with one another to estimate whole squares.

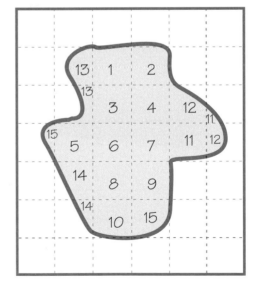

   A. How many whole squares did he count?

   B. Find the two pieces he "put together" to make square number 15. Do you agree they make about a whole square centimeter?

   C. What is Professor Peabody's estimate for the area?

The Better "Picker Upper"

Professor Peabody Finds the Better "Picker Upper"

While working in his lab, Professor Peabody knocked over a graduated cylinder filled with water. He grabbed a roll of paper towels and used several sheets to clean up the spill. Professor Peabody thought, "These paper towels don't soak up very much water. The brand I use at home works better."

Professor Peabody decided to investigate different brands of paper towels to find which is the better "picker upper."

I. What does it mean to be the better "picker upper"?

The next day Professor Peabody brought two different brands of paper towels to the lab. He wanted to compare these two with the roll he had in his lab. He tore off one sheet from each roll and compared them.

2. Your teacher has three different brands of paper towels. Compare the three brands. How are they alike? How are they different?

Professor Peabody investigated further by dropping a few drops of water on a sheet of each brand of paper towel.

3. Will the spots be the same size?

4. A. How can he measure the size of the spots?
   B. Which variable will give the best measure of the size: length, width, or area?

Professor Peabody decided to use the TIMS Laboratory Method to help him find the better "picker upper." You will do a similar experiment.

5. What two main variables will you study?

6. What will you have to keep the same during the experiment in order for your investigation to be fair? (What variables do you need to keep fixed?)

Using Number Sense at the Book Sale

Sheena's class is having a used book sale. The books for sale are listed on the next page. For most of the problems you will not need an exact answer, so try to solve the problems in your head. Be ready to explain your methods to the class.

I have $2. I want to buy *Superfudge, Mr. Popper's Penguins,* and *James and the Giant Peach.* 2 dollars is the same as 8 quarters. *Superfudge* is 50¢, or 2 quarters. *Mr. Popper's Penguins* is 1 quarter, and *James and the Giant Peach* costs 75 cents, or 3 quarters. That's 6 quarters altogether. I have more than enough money!

Price List

Title	Author	Price
Betsy-Tacy	Maud Hart Lovelace	20¢
Mr. Popper's Penguins	Richard and Florence Atwater	25¢
Ramón Makes a Trade	Barbara Ritchie	45¢
Superfudge	Judy Blume	50¢
Fudge-a-mania	Judy Blume	50¢
Charlie and the Chocolate Factory	Roald Dahl	75¢
James and the Giant Peach	Roald Dahl	75¢
Ramona Quimby, Age 8	Beverly Cleary	95¢
Ramona and Her Father	Beverly Cleary	95¢
Children of the Fire	Harriette Gillem Robinet	$1.00
Amazing Grace	Mary Hoffman	$1.50
Little House Books	Laura Ingalls Wilder	4 for $1.00

1. Pretend you are going to the book store with quarters.
   A. Do you need three or four quarters to buy *Ramona Quimby, Age 8?*
   B. How many quarters do you need to buy *Betsy-Tacy?*

2. Susie has $1.00. Can she buy *Ramón Makes a Trade* and *Superfudge?* Why or why not?

3. James has $1.00. Can he buy *Betsy-Tacy, Mr. Popper's Penguins,* and *Fudge-a-mania?* Why or why not?

4. Tino has $1.25. Does he have enough money to buy *Ramón Makes a Trade* and *Ramona and Her Father?* Why or why not?

5. Terrell has $2.00. Can he buy both books by Roald Dahl and *Fudge-a-mania?* Why or why not?

6. Sheena has $3.00. She wants to buy both the books by Beverly Cleary and *Amazing Grace*. Does she have enough money? Why or why not?

7. Liz has $4.00. She wants to buy the books listed below. Does she have enough money? Why or why not?

   Betsy-Tacy   *Mr. Popper's Penguins*

   Superfudge   *Fudge-a-mania*

   James and the Giant Peach   *Children of the Fire*

8. Ana has $2.50. If she buys *Children of the Fire* and *Charlie and the Chocolate Factory,* how many *Little House* books can she buy?

9. If you had $4.00, which books would you buy? Make a list and describe how you made your choices. Tell how you know that you will have enough money. You can use pictures, words, or number sentences.

Unit 6

More Adding and Subtracting

	Student Guide	Discovery Assignment Book	Adventure Book	Unit Resource Guide*
Lesson 1				
The 500 Hats				
Lesson 2				
The Coat of Many Bits	◎			
Lesson 3				
Adding with Base-Ten Pieces	◎	◎		
Lesson 4				
Subtracting with Base-Ten Pieces	◎	◎		
Lesson 5				
Close Enough!	◎			◎
Lesson 6				
Leonardo the Blockhead			◎	
Lesson 7				
Palindromes				
Lesson 8				
Digits Game		◎		

Unit Resource Guide pages are from the teacher materials.

The Coat of Many Bits

Making Costumes for a Play

Help wanted! Your creative talents are needed to help make costumes for the school play "Michael and the Land of Many Colors." The students want to cover the front of the costumes with a special, colorful material. They need your help in figuring out how much of this material they will need. To do this, your group will need one coat.

1. Trace the outline of the coat onto a large piece of paper.

2. Use base-ten pieces to find out how much material (in square centimeters) will be needed to cover the front of your group's coat. Use any shortcuts that will save time in finding this area.

3. Write the area of your coat on a piece of paper or an index card.

4. Make a list of the areas of all of the coats in the class in order from smallest to largest.

5. Do the problems below. Make sure that your answers are reasonable.

   A. About how much bigger is the largest coat than the smallest coat?

   B. Is it more or less than 500 square centimeters bigger?

   C. Is it more or less than 1000 square centimeters bigger?

6. If the material costs 10¢ for every 100 square centimeters, how much will it cost to cover your group's coat? Show how you found your answer.

7. When you made your costumes, your group started with a big piece of material and then cut out just enough material to cover your group's coat. If the original piece of material had a total area of 6000 square centimeters, about how much would be left over after you cut out enough material to cover your group's coat?

Adding with Base-Ten Pieces

Trading with Base-Ten Pieces

Nikia and Maruta work at the TIMS Candy Company. On Monday, Nikia made 257 Chocos. Maruta made 668 Chocos. Using base-ten shorthand they found the amount of candy they made together on a *Base-Ten Board*. Look carefully at each box.

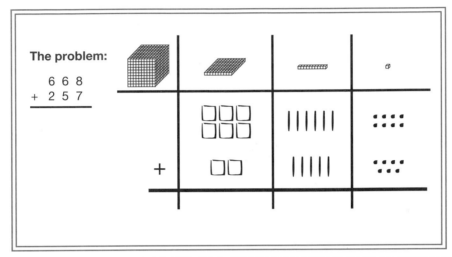

The problem:

```
    6 6 8
  + 2 5 7
  _____
```

a. Combine each column.

b. 10 skinnies can be traded for 1 flat.

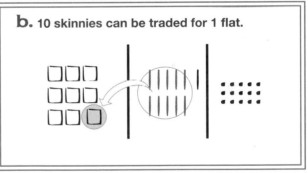

c. 10 bits can be traded for 1 skinny.

d. What is the answer?

```
    6 6 8
  + 2 5 7
  _____
```

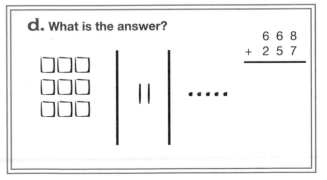

1. Describe what Nikia and Maruta did to solve the problem.

2. Nikia started to record her work with the pieces. Copy her work on a *Base-Ten Recording Sheet.* Using the Fewest Pieces Rule, show how 8 flats, 11 skinnies, and 15 bits will match Nikia and Maruta's answer.

	6	**6**	**8**
+	**2**	**5**	**7**
	8	**11**	**15**

After work on Tuesday, Nikia and Maruta wanted to find out how many Chocos they made together. Nikia made more Chocos than Maruta this time. They set up the problem like this:

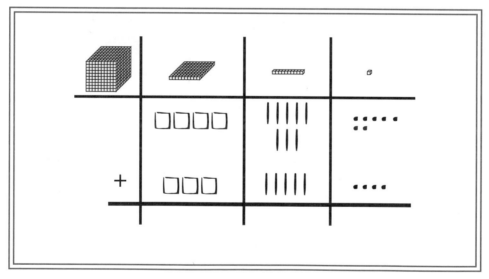

3. How many Chocos did Nikia make?

4. How many did Maruta make?

5. Use base-ten pieces and a *Base-Ten Board* to find the total amount of Chocos Maruta and Nikia made on Tuesday.

More Shortcut Addition

Kris has worked at the TIMS Candy Company for a long time. Kris knows that it is not necessary to use the record sheet when adding if the Fewest Pieces Rule is used and only 1 digit is written in each column.

He showed his shortcut method to Andy.

$$
\begin{array}{r}
\overset{1}{5}4 \\
+\ 47 \\
\hline
101
\end{array}
$$

6. Why did Kris put the 1 above the 5? What does the 1 mean?

Andy tried a problem, too.

$$
\begin{array}{r}
\overset{1}{6}\overset{1}{4}7 \\
+\ 285 \\
\hline
932
\end{array}
$$

7. Why did Andy put a 1 above the 4? What does the 1 mean?

8. Why did Andy put a 1 above the 6? What does that 1 mean?

Now try this problem:

$$
\begin{array}{r}
435 \\
+\ 168 \\
\hline
\end{array}
$$

Katie, Scott, and Nora solved the problem using paper and pencil. Here is their work.

Katie's solution	Scott's solution	Nora's solution
$\begin{array}{r}\overset{1}{4}\overset{1}{3}5 \\ +\ 168 \\ \hline 603\end{array}$	$\begin{array}{r}435 \\ +\ 1\overset{1}{6}8 \\ \hline 603\end{array}$	$\begin{array}{r}435 \\ +\ 168 \\ \hline 13 \\ 90 \\ 500 \\ \hline 603\end{array}$

9. Compare the three pencil-and-paper solutions. Explain what Katie, Scott, and Nora did to find their answers.

Adding with Base-Ten Pieces

Homework

Do the following problems using a shortcut method. You may use base-ten shorthand if you wish.

1.
$$\begin{array}{r} 68 \\ + 39 \\ \hline \end{array}$$

2.
$$\begin{array}{r} 403 \\ + 79 \\ \hline \end{array}$$

3.
$$\begin{array}{r} 247 \\ + 130 \\ \hline \end{array}$$

4.
$$\begin{array}{r} 1235 \\ + 2638 \\ \hline \end{array}$$

5.
$$\begin{array}{r} 5762 \\ + 1829 \\ \hline \end{array}$$

6.
$$\begin{array}{r} 3209 \\ + 5732 \\ \hline \end{array}$$

7. Explain a way to solve Question 2 in your head.

8. Explain a way to solve Question 6 in your head.

9. Andy and Kris made 1432 Chocos on Wednesday, 938 Chocos on Thursday, and 2007 Chocos on Friday. Put these numbers in order from smallest to largest.

10. How many Chocos did they make altogether on Wednesday and Thursday?

Subtracting with Base-Ten Pieces

Selling Chocos

At the end of each day, employees at the TIMS Candy Company Store find out how many Chocos are left on the shelves.

1. At the start of one day the store had 573 Chocos. During the day 289 Chocos were sold. The manager asked Beth to find out how many Chocos were left. Describe each step Beth took to solve the problem.

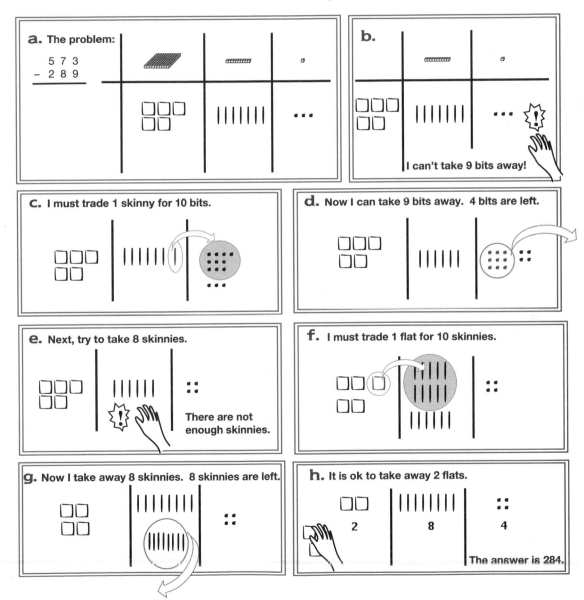

a. The problem:
$$573 - 289$$

b. I can't take 9 bits away!

c. I must trade 1 skinny for 10 bits.

d. Now I can take 9 bits away. 4 bits are left.

e. Next, try to take 8 skinnies. There are not enough skinnies.

f. I must trade 1 flat for 10 skinnies.

g. Now I take away 8 skinnies. 8 skinnies are left.

h. It is ok to take away 2 flats.
2   8   4
The answer is 284.

2. Beth recorded her work on a recording sheet. Discuss how her work here matches the work with the base-ten pieces. How can you tell that she traded 1 skinny for 10 bits? Did she trade 1 flat for 10 skinnies? How do you know? How did she take away 8 skinnies?

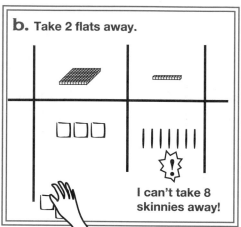

Alex solved the problem differently. Compare it to Beth's approach.

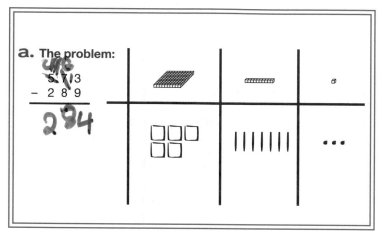

a. The problem:

$$\begin{array}{r} 5\,7\,3 \\ -\ 2\,8\,9 \\ \hline 2\,8\,4 \end{array}$$

b. Take 2 flats away.

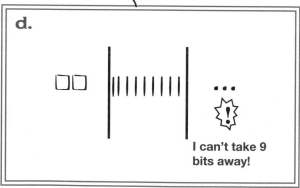

I can't take 8 skinnies away!

c. I must trade 1 flat for 10 skinnies.

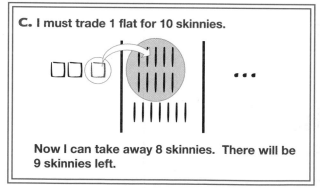

Now I can take away 8 skinnies. There will be 9 skinnies left.

d.

I can't take 9 bits away!

e. I must trade 1 skinny for 10 bits.

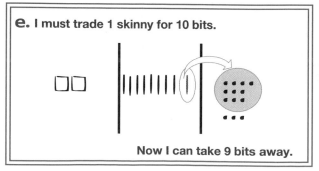

Now I can take 9 bits away.

f. The answer is...

| | 2 | 8 | 4 |

3. Alex started to show his work on a recording sheet. Copy his work on a *Base-Ten Recording Sheet.* Finish the problem for Alex. Look at his work with the base-ten pieces to help you.

	5	7	3
−	2	8	9
	3		

Shortcut Subtraction

Maruta learned the shortcut method for addition. She then figured out a way to subtract without using the *Base-Ten Recording Sheet*. This means she always used the Fewest Pieces Rule.

Here is how Maruta did 476 − 143.

$$\begin{array}{r} 476 \\ -\ 143 \\ \hline 333 \end{array}$$

Nikia tried her method to solve 536 − 218, but she had to regroup.

I have to take 8 bits from 6 bits. That's impossible. I'll have to regroup. I can take a skinny and trade it for 10 bits. Then I will have enough bits to subtract.

$$\begin{array}{r} \overset{2\ \ 16}{5\cancel{3}6} \\ -\ 218 \\ \hline 318 \end{array}$$

4. Explain why Maruta wrote the 4 above the 5 and 16 above the 6 in the problem below.

$$\begin{array}{r} \overset{4\ 16}{756} \\ -\ 167 \\ \hline 9 \end{array}$$

5. Maruta continued the problem. Explain why she wrote a 6 above the 7 and a 14 above the 4.

$$\begin{array}{r} \overset{\overset{14}{6\ \ \overset{\!\!4}{\ }16}}{756} \\ -\ 167 \\ \hline 589 \end{array}$$

Dime Store Problems

Art's Dime Store is a favorite for many third graders. It has almost anything a third grader would want, and the people who work there are friendly to kids.

Art's Dime Store sells LOTS of penny candy (candy that costs only 1¢). The table below shows how much penny candy the store sold in the first four months of the year.

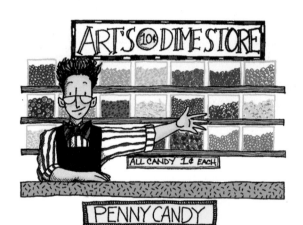

6. How much penny candy did the store sell in January and February together?

7. The store sold lots of candy in February because Valentine's Day is February 14. How much more penny candy did the store sell in February than in January?

8. The biggest month for selling penny candy is October because that's when Halloween is. Art thinks that he will sell as much candy in October as he did in March and April combined. How much candy should Art order for October?

Month	Number of Pieces of Candy Sold
January	2394
February	5620
March	3306
April	4885

9. Make up and solve your own problems about penny candy sales at Art's Dime Store.

10. Art's Dime Store has four large tanks of goldfish. Here are Art's inventory records for the goldfish last week:

Number of goldfish at beginning of week	588
Number of new goldfish Art bought from his supplier	603
Number of goldfish sold to customers	462
Number of goldfish that died	81

At the end of the week, did Art have more goldfish or fewer goldfish in the tanks than he had at the beginning of the week? Explain.

Art has to keep careful records of all his sales. Here are the daily total sales for the store during the first week in April.

Day of the Week Sale	Sales (in dollars)
Monday	5271
Tuesday	3008
Wednesday	3065
Thursday	4753
Friday	4329
Saturday	8297
Sunday	6084

11. The busiest days for the store are usually on the weekend. What were the sales for Saturday and Sunday together?

12. How much more were the combined sales of Saturday and Sunday than the combined sales of the next two busiest days?

13. During the same week last year, the store's sales on Tuesday were $2862. How much more did Art's Dime Store sell this year on Tuesday?

14. Make up and solve your own problems about sales at Art's Dime Store.

Homework

Do the following problems using a shortcut subtraction method. You may use base-ten shorthand to help you if you wish.

1.
$$\begin{array}{r} 687 \\ -49 \\ \hline \end{array}$$

2.
$$\begin{array}{r} 4327 \\ -263 \\ \hline \end{array}$$

3.
$$\begin{array}{r} 3067 \\ -1478 \\ \hline \end{array}$$

4.
$$\begin{array}{r} 2056 \\ -1689 \\ \hline \end{array}$$

5.
$$\begin{array}{r} 1003 \\ -999 \\ \hline \end{array}$$

6.
$$\begin{array}{r} 489 \\ -301 \\ \hline \end{array}$$

7. Explain a way to do problem 5 in your head.

8. Explain a way to do problem 6 in your head.

Close Enough!

That's Close Enough

Three schools are getting together for a sports day at Longfellow School. There are 247 students from Longfellow School, 457 from Clark School, and 322 from Lincoln School. Sam, a third grader at Longfellow School, says he thinks there were about 1050 students at the sports day. His classmates discussed his estimate.

Reanin said, "Well, I'll add the hundreds first."

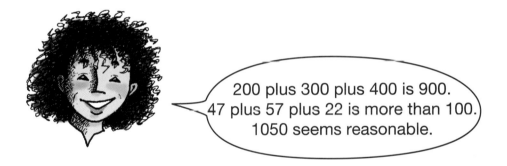

200 plus 300 plus 400 is 900.
47 plus 57 plus 22 is more than 100.
1050 seems reasonable.

Lenny said, "I think of it a different way."

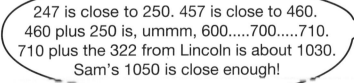

247 is close to 250. 457 is close to 460.
460 plus 250 is, ummm, 600.....700.....710.
710 plus the 322 from Lincoln is about 1030.
Sam's 1050 is close enough!

Nell said, "It's easier for me to work with 50 instead of 47 and 57."

247 and 457 is about 700.
700 and 322 is 1022.
I agree with Sam's estimate too.

1. Discuss the problem. How would you find a good estimate? Do you think Sam's estimate is reasonable?

2. The Lincoln coach compared sports day this year to last year. More students participated last year. Last year there were 312 students from Longfellow School, 542 from Clark School, and 365 from Lincoln School. What is a reasonable estimate for the number of students who attended sports day last year? Explain how you decided.

3. For each number, give the closest ten and the closest hundred. The first one is done for you.

   A. 284   The closest ten is 280.   The closest hundred is 300.

   B. 128

   C. 421

   D. 910

   E. 203

   F. 685

   G. 550

   H. 805

   I. 369

   J. 1502

Producing the Play

Homework

The following problems arose when the teachers and students were producing the play "Michael and the Land of Many Colors." Help them by solving the problems.

Estimate an answer. Then, solve the problem. Decide if your answer is reasonable. Explain how you solved the problem.

1. For opening night of the play, the students in two classes decorated the auditorium with balloons. Ms. Angelo's class used 156 balloons. Mr. Sullivan's class used 138 balloons.

   A. Estimate the total number of balloons blown up by the two classes. Do you think the total is closer to 200, 300, or 400? Why?

   B. Exactly how many balloons did they blow up?

2. In the play, Silvia and Mario each hold a teddy bear. The front of each teddy bear needs to be covered with fancy material. Silvia measured her teddy bear and found that it needed 1235 square centimeters of fancy material. Mario measured his teddy bear and found that it needed 73 square centimeters more than Silvia's bear.

   A. Estimate the amount of material needed for Mario's bear. Is it closest to 1200, 1250, or 1300 square centimeters?

   B. Exactly how much material did Mario's bear need?

3. To make the scenery, they had to measure the distance across the stage. Naomi and Dave measured the stage together. Naomi began measuring from the right side and Dave from the left. When they met, Naomi had measured 327 cm and Dave had measured 273 cm. What is the distance across the stage?

---

4. Students sold tickets to two performances of the play. By the day of the play, students had sold 385 advance tickets for the first performance. They sold 656 advance tickets for both performances combined.

   A. Do you think that more tickets were sold for the first performance or the second performance? Why?

   B. How many tickets were sold for the second performance?

   C. If the auditorium has 400 seats, how many tickets will they have left to sell at the door at each of the two performances?

5. The students held a bake sale to raise extra money to pay for the scenery and costumes. Students in Mr. Sullivan's and Ms. Angelo's classes brought in cookies for the bake sale. Ms. Angelo's class brought in 194 cookies and Mr. Sullivan's class brought in 235.

   A. If Ms. Angelo's class brought in 100 more cookies, would they have more cookies than Mr. Sullivan's class?

   B. How many extra cookies would Ms. Angelo's class need to have the same number as Mr. Sullivan's class?

6. The bake sale earned $253. Students used $185 to buy material for the costumes.

   A. After buying the material for the costumes, did the students have more or less than $100 left from the bake sale money?

   B. Exactly how much money did they have left?

7. Solve the following problems using any method you choose. Estimate to be sure your answer is reasonable.

   A.
   $$377 + 451$$

   B.
   $$621 - 557$$

   C.
   $$805 - 626$$

8. Explain your estimation strategy for Question 7B.

Unit 7
Exploring Multiplication and Division

	Student Guide	Discovery Assignment Book	Adventure Book	Unit Resource Guide*
Lesson 1				
Lemonade Stand		◎		
Lesson 2				
Katie's Job				◎
Lesson 3				
Mathhoppers	◎	◎		
Lesson 4				
Birthday Party	◎			
Lesson 5				
The Money Jar	◎			◎
Lesson 6				
Walking around Shapes		◎		◎

Unit Resource Guide pages are from the teacher materials.

Lemonade Stand

Maria and Daniel decided to earn some money by selling lemonade. They tried different recipes for fresh lemonade until they decided upon their favorite.

Homemade Lemonade

Ingredients
Juice from 8 lemons
2 quarts of cold water
1 cup sugar

Instructions
1. Combine all ingredients in a large (2-quart) pitcher.
2. Stir well so that the sugar dissolves (mixes in) completely.
3. Pour over ice cubes.

Makes one 2-quart pitcher.

1. Maria and Daniel already have all the sugar and water they need, but they have to buy lemons. Make a table like the one below, and use the recipe to fill in the missing data. What patterns do you see in your data table?

P Number of Pitchers	L Number of Lemons
1	
2	
4	
8	

2. Make a bar graph of the data. Number the horizontal axis by ones to at least 12. Number the vertical axis by fours to at least 80. What patterns do you see on your graph?

3. How many lemons do Maria and Daniel need to make six pitchers of lemonade? Explain how you found your answer.

A bar graph is a good way to make a picture of your data. But scientists and mathematicians also use point graphs.

4. To change your bar graph to a point graph, make a big dot at the top of each bar. Do your dots form a pattern?

5. Can you use your ruler to draw a line through the dots? Try it. Draw your line to the end of the graph in both directions.

This is part of Maria and Daniel's graph. The beginning of your graph should look the same.

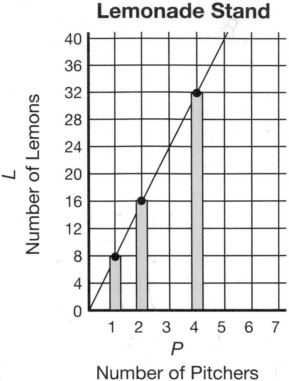

Lemonade Stand

Use your graph to solve Questions 6, 7, 8, and 9. Draw dashed lines on your graph to show how you found each answer. Then, solve the problem another way to check your answer. Explain how you checked your answer.

6. How many lemons do Maria and Daniel need to make five pitchers of lemonade?

7. How many lemons do they need to make ten pitchers of lemonade?

8. How many pitchers of lemonade can they make with 72 lemons?

9. How many pitchers of lemonade can they make with 44 lemons?

10. Make up problems like Questions 6, 7, 8, and 9. Give your problems to another student to solve.

Use this chart to help you solve Questions 11, 12, and 13. Explain how you found your answers.

Ingredient	Cost
Lemons	50¢ each
Sugar	25¢ per cup
Paper Cup	3¢ each
Water	free

One pitcher of lemonade makes 8 servings.

11. How much does it cost to make and sell one pitcher of lemonade?

12. What should be the price of one serving of lemonade?

13. If Maria and Daniel use this price, how much lemonade do they need to sell to make a $2 profit?

Mathhoppers

Mathhoppers are very special creatures that live on number lines. Every time a mathhopper hops, it hops the same distance.

Professor Peabody studies the behavior of mathhoppers. He has found several kinds of mathhoppers, including the +3 ("plus three") mathhopper. The +3 mathhopper always hops 3 units to the right on the number line. He observed a +3 mathhopper start at 0 and hop four times. Where did it land?

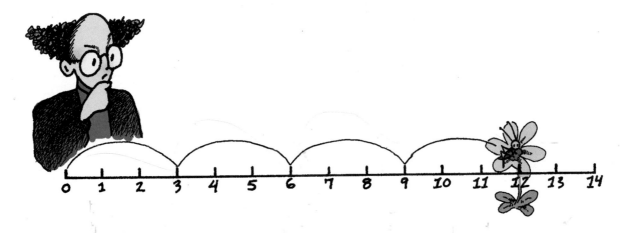

He also discovered that mathhoppers do not have to start at 0. He watched a +2 mathhopper start at 3 and hop 5 times. Where did it land?

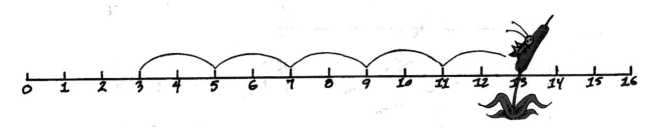

In fact, mathhoppers do not have to hop to the right on the number line. Professor Peabody found a –1 ("minus one") mathhopper, which hops 1 unit to the left on the number line. It started at ten and hopped 6 times. Where did it land?

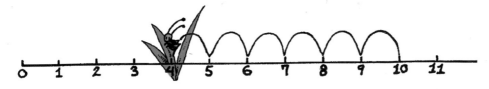

1. A +2 mathhopper started at 0 and hopped 4 times. On what number did it land? How did you find your answer?

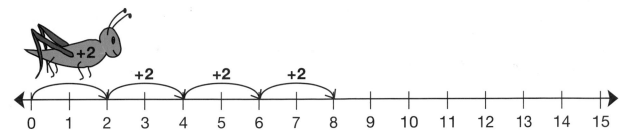

2. A +5 mathhopper started at 0 and hopped 3 times. On what number did it land? Explain how you found your answer.

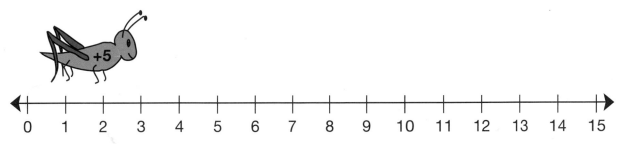

3. A +10 mathhopper started at 0 and hopped 3 times. On what number did it land? Write a number sentence to explain what the mathhopper did.

4. A +$\frac{1}{2}$ mathhopper started at 0 and hopped 4 times. On what number did it land? Write a number sentence to explain what the mathhopper did. Explain how you found your answer.

5. A +$\frac{1}{2}$ mathhopper started at 0 and hopped 5 times. Where did it land? Write a number sentence to explain what the mathhopper did. Explain how you found your answer.

6. A +4 mathhopper started at 0 and hopped 5 times. On what number did it land? Write a number sentence to explain what the mathhopper did.

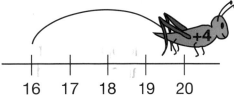

7. A +4 mathhopper started at 0 and hopped until it reached 20. How many hops did it take? Explain.

8. A +2 mathhopper started at 0 and hopped until it reached 14. How many hops did it take? Explain.

9. A +8 mathhopper started at 0 and hopped until it reached 40. How many hops did it take? Explain.

18 19 20

10. A mathhopper started at 0 and hopped 5 times. It ended up at 20. How big were its hops? Explain.

11. A mathhopper started at 0 and hopped 6 times. It landed on 60. How big were its hops? Explain.

12. Make up two mathhopper problems. Trade problems with another group, and see if you can answer their problems. When they have finished answering your problems, you can check their answers.

13. Suppose we have a +5 mathhopper that started at 2. Where did it land if it hopped 3 times? Write a number sentence to explain your answer.

14. A +3 mathhopper started at 3 and hopped 6 times. Where did it land? Write a number sentence to explain what the mathhopper did.

15. A +10 mathhopper started at 3 and hopped 4 times. Where did it land? Write a number sentence to explain what the mathhopper did.

16. A +5 mathhopper started at 10 and hopped 8 times. Where did it land? Write a number sentence to explain what the mathhopper did.

17. A −2 mathhopper started at 10 and hopped 3 times. Where did it land? Write a number sentence to explain what the mathhopper did.

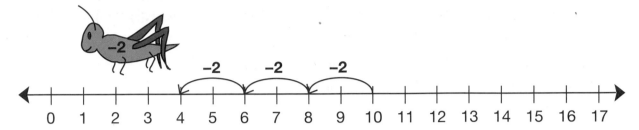

18. A −2 mathhopper started at 10 and hopped 5 times. Where did it land? Write a number sentence to explain what the mathhopper did.

19. A −4 mathhopper started at 24 and hopped 6 times. Where did it land? Write a number sentence to explain what the mathhopper did.

20. A −4 mathhopper started at 26 and hopped 6 times. Where did it land? Write a number sentence to explain what the mathhopper did.

21. A −10 mathhopper started at 47 and hopped 3 times. Where did it land? Write a number sentence to explain what the mathhopper did.

22. A mathhopper started at 35. It hopped 7 times and landed on 0. What kind of mathhopper is it? Explain your answer.

Birthday Party

Tina is planning her birthday party. She has invited 14 friends. Since she will also be there, she will plan the party for 15 people. Use counters to solve the following problems. You may also draw pictures or write number sentences. For each problem, explain how you found your answer.

Use these 30 pennies to help you figure out how to divide the cupcakes among your guests. Each penny will stand for one cupcake.

I want to be fair. Everyone should get the same amount.

1. Tina plans to use tables that seat four people. How many tables will she need?

2. She will make 30 cupcakes. If the cupcakes are divided equally, how many cupcakes will each person get?

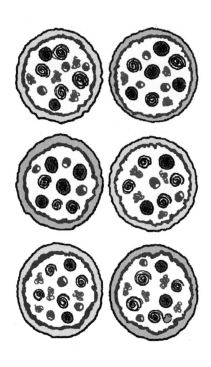

After getting the invitations, three friends called Tina and said they could not come.

3. Now, for how many people must she plan?

4. How many tables will she now need?

5. How will she divide the cupcakes now?

6. Tina also plans to order six pizzas to serve for lunch. If she shares all the pizza equally, how much pizza will each person get?

7. Tina wants to put a set of 28 dominoes on each table so that each table can play a game. If all four players get the same number of dominoes, how many dominoes will each player get?

Homework

At the end of Tina's birthday party, she will give each of her guests a party bag. After she fills the bags with toys and candy, she will tie the bags with ribbon. She bought 45 inches of red ribbon and one yard of blue ribbon.

To help you answer the following questions, you should use a yardstick or ruler, scissors, and ribbon or string. You may wish to use pictures, number sentences, or words. For each problem, explain how you found your answer.

1. If Tina cuts the red ribbon into pieces that are 7 inches long, how many pieces of red ribbon will she have?

2. She cut the blue ribbon into four equal pieces. How long is each piece?

3. Tina needs two more pieces of ribbon. She found one piece of green ribbon that is 17 inches long and cut it into two equal pieces. How long is each piece?

The Money Jar

The Franklins save their pennies, nickels, and dimes in a jar in the family room. The father, Frank, and the mother, Flora, have four children—Frankie Franklin, Fred Franklin, Fern Franklin, and Ben Franklin. On the first Friday of each month, the Franklins divide the coins in the jar among the members of the family according to the following rules:

- The children always share the pennies equally.
- The dimes are divided equally among all the members of the family.
- Any money that cannot be divided equally is put back into the jar.

Write number sentences to show how you solved the problems.

1. In April, they counted 48 pennies in the jar.
   A. How many pennies did each child get?
   B. How many pennies did they put back in the jar?

2. In May, there were 38 pennies in the jar.
   A. How many pennies did each child get?
   B. How many pennies did they put back in the jar?

3. In February, there were five children in the house because the Franklins' friend Farley visited. If each child got 12 pennies, how many pennies were in the jar?

4. In April, they counted 48 dimes.
   A. How many dimes did each person get?
   B. How much money did each person get?
   C. How much money did they put back in the jar?

5. In May, there were 31 dimes in the jar.
   A. How much money did each person get?
   B. How much money did they put back in the jar?

6. In June, there were 15 dimes.
   A. How much money did each person get?
   B. How much money did they put back in the jar?

7. In February, there were 42 dimes. (Don't forget that Farley was visiting in February!)
   A. How much money did each person get?
   B. How much money did they put back in the jar?

8. In July, there were 18 dimes and 19 pennies.
   A. How much money did each family member get?
   B. How much money was put back in the jar?

9. If there were 24 pennies in the jar in August, would there be pennies to put back in the jar for September? Explain.

Homework

Your family decides to save coins in a money jar and to divide them evenly among the members of your family each month. One month, your family finds 36 dimes in the jar. How much money will each member of your family get? How much money will be left over? Write a number sentence to show your solution to the problem. You can solve this problem at home using counters of some sort, such as beans, checkers, or toothpicks.

Unit 8

MAPPING AND COORDINATES

	Student Guide	Discovery Assignment Book	Adventure Book	Unit Resource Guide*
Lesson 1				
Meet Mr. Origin				
Lesson 2				
Sara's Desk	◎			◎
Lesson 3				
Mapping a Tiny TIMS Town	◎	◎		◎
Lesson 4				
The Ghost Galleons			◎	
Lesson 5				
Tens Game	◎			
Lesson 6				
Tall Buildings	◎			

Unit Resource Guide pages are from the teacher materials.

Meet Mr. Origin

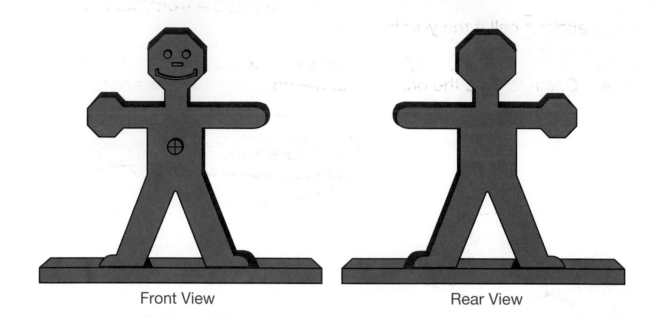

Front View   Rear View

This is Mr. Origin.

Does your Mr. Origin look the same as this one? This Mr. Origin has a glove on his right hand. What is special about the right hand of your Mr. Origin?

We can use Mr. Origin to help describe where things are. We can draw a line through Mr. Origin that goes from left to right. We call that the **left/right axis**. (Mr. Origin's hands point to the left/right axis.) Mathematicians call it the **x-axis**.

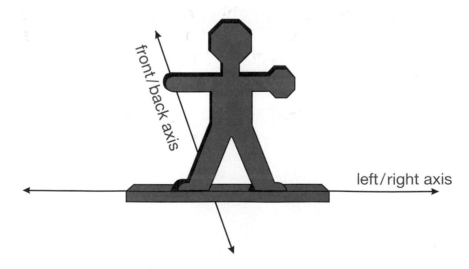

Mr. Origin has a button on his front with a + on it. We can draw a line through Mr. Origin that goes from front to back. We call that the **front/back axis.** Mathematicians call it the **y-axis.**

You can use Mr. Origin to map the objects in your classroom. Sara and José used Mr. Origin to map the positions of the desk and the wastebasket.

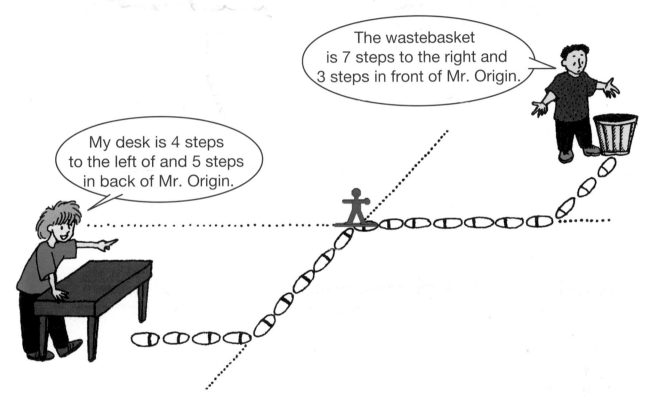

The wastebasket is 7 steps to the right and 3 steps in front of Mr. Origin.

My desk is 4 steps to the left of and 5 steps in back of Mr. Origin.

José's wastebasket is 7 steps to the right of and 3 steps in front of Mr. Origin. The **coordinates** of the wastebasket's location are 7 steps right and 3 steps front. Sara's desk is 4 steps to the left of and 5 steps in back of Mr. Origin. What are the coordinates of Sara's desk?

Sara and José measured using steps. They could also have measured with standard units of measure like feet or meters.

Measuring with Mr. Origin

Use your Mr. Origin to map some objects in your classroom. Find a place for your group's Mr. Origin, and tape him down.

Choose at least three objects in your classroom. Work with your group to find the coordinates for each object, and write them in a data table like the one below.

Classroom Coordinates

Object	Right/Left (in _____)	Front/Back (in _____)

Trade data tables with another group. Check their data using their Mr. Origin. If you think they made an error, discuss it with them. They may decide to change their data.

Sara's Desk

Here is a map of Sara's desk.

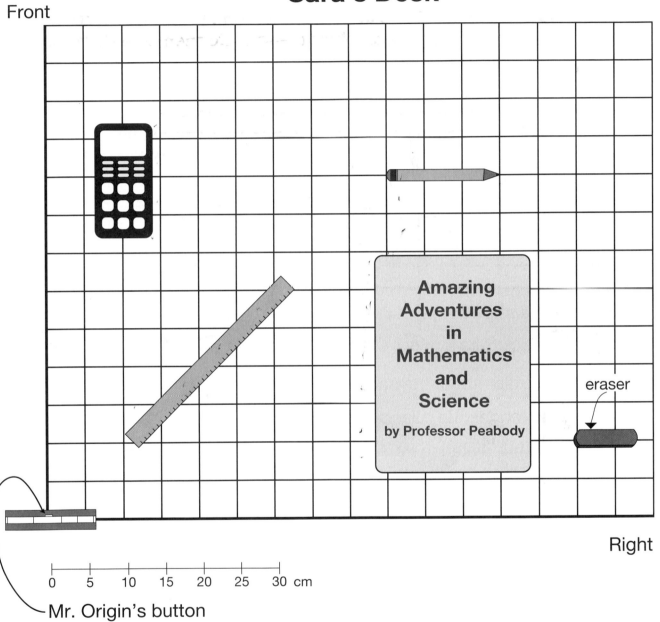

Sara's Desk

Front

Amazing
Adventures
in
Mathematics
and
Science

by Professor Peabody

eraser

Right

0   5   10   15   20   25   30 cm

Mr. Origin's button

Discuss these questions with your class.

1. Each centimeter on the map stands for what distance in the real world?

2. Where is Mr. Origin on the map? Why does Mr. Origin look like a rectangle on the map? Can you see his button?

3. How long is Sara's pencil? Explain how you found your answer.

4. How long is Sara's calculator? Does that seem right? Is it about the same length as your calculator?

5. Which is longer, the pencil or the calculator?

6. About how far is it from the pencil to the edge of the book?

Discuss these questions with your group. Then, write answers to these questions on a sheet of paper.

7. How long is Sara's ruler? Describe more than one way to find out.

8. Is Sara's ruler about the same length as your ruler?

9. Which is longer, the ruler or the book? Tell how you know.

10. Estimate the distance from the bottom of the calculator to the closest corner of the book. Then, find the exact distance. Was your estimate close?

11. About how wide is the calculator?

12. Do you think the grid is helpful in mapping Sara's desk? Why?

Using a book, calculator, pencil, eraser, and ruler, try to make your desk look like Sara's desk.

Find the Panda

Professor Peabody is helping to preserve pandas, which are an endangered species. Pandas are very good at hiding, however. When Professor Peabody first found his panda, he put a radio collar on the panda. That way, he would be able to locate the panda to give it a yearly health checkup.

In this game, you will use the information from the radio collar—given in front and right coordinates—to help Professor Peabody find the panda as quickly as possible. Here's how you play:

1. One player is the panda. The other player is Professor Peabody's helper.

2. Each player needs one copy of the *Find the Panda Game Board*.

3. The player who is the panda marks the location of the panda on his or her game board. This player must keep the location a secret.

4. The other player helps Professor Peabody find the panda by guessing its coordinates. This player and the panda plot each guess on his or her own game board.

5. After each guess, the panda must give a clue to the other player. The clue must tell the other player which direction he or she needs to go from the last guess.

If you play additional games, you can take turns being the panda.

Marco is the panda. He has chosen 3 right, 12 front as the location of the panda. Jackie, one of Professor Peabody's helpers, guesses 7 right, 8 front. Jackie records the guess on her game board.

Marco records the guess on his game board too. He sees that Jackie must go left and front to reach the panda. So, he says, "Go left and front."

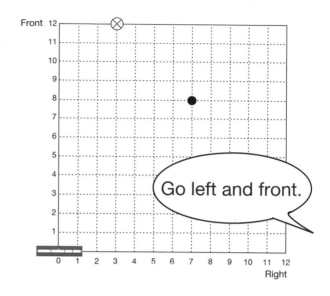

Marco's game board

Jackie guesses again. This time she guesses 3 right, 8 front. Here is Jackie's game board. It shows both of her guesses. Is Jackie's second guess a good guess? Why or why not?

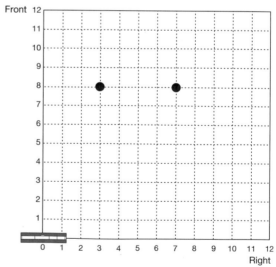

Jackie's game board

Marco says, "Now go front." Why did he say this?

If you were playing the game and didn't know where the panda was, what would be your next guess?

Mapping a Tiny TIMS Town

Professor Peabody fell asleep and imagined he landed on a planet far, far away.

He dreamed that he landed at a place called TIMS Town. The people there were less than 1 centimeter tall. It was a tiny TIMS Town.

Setting Up Your Tiny TIMS Town

You are going to build your own tiny TIMS town using connecting cubes. We will give you the floor plans for four buildings: a school, a library, a market, and a bank.

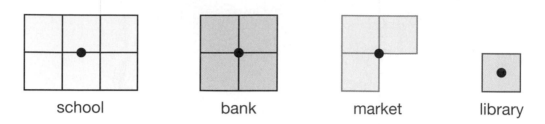

school   bank   market   library

Marcus and Maria made four buildings from these floor plans. Here are drawings of their school, bank, library, and market. Can you tell which one is the bank, the library, the school, and the market?

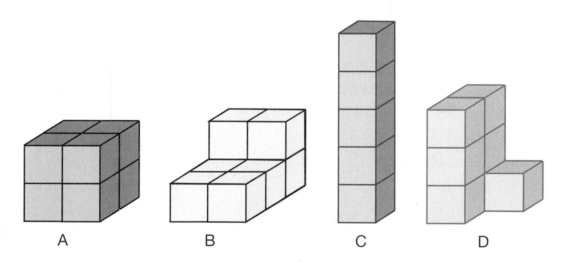

A   B   C   D

Use centimeter connecting cubes to make your own school, library, market, and bank. You should use the floor plans we have given you for these buildings, but your buildings can be different from Marcus and Maria's.

Before you place the buildings in your town, you need to put Mr. Origin in the corner of your town so that you will be able to make a map of it later. Be sure he is facing the correct direction. His right arm should be parallel to one of the tape measures.

Now, you are ready to put your buildings in the town. Here is a picture of the TIMS Town that Marcus and Maria made.

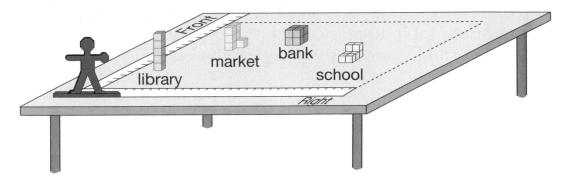

Cut out floor plans for each of your buildings from *Tape Measures for TIMS Town.* Place a dot in the center of each floor plan. Glue or tape the floor plans down in the positions you chose for your buildings. When you are done, your town will be finished.

Mapping Your Town

Use a ruler to find the coordinates for all your buildings. Make all measurements to the dot in the center of your building floor plans. Put the data in a data table like the one below.

Building	Right (in _____)	Front (in _____)
library		
market		
bank		
school		

Use a piece of graph paper to make a map of your tiny TIMS town. First, you will need to decide how to number the axes.

Then, you can draw in your buildings. For each building, you can begin by using your data table to mark its center on the map with a dot. Using the dot as the center, you can then sketch the building's floor plan around it.

Using Your Town Map

1. Using only your map and a ruler, predict the actual distances (as the crow flies) between the buildings in your TIMS Town. Measure to the center of each building. Use a data table like the one below, and enter your predictions under "Predicted Distance Using the Map."

Building	Predicted Distance Using the Map (in ———)	Actual Distance in TIMS Town (in ———)	Error (in ———)
bank to market			
market to school			
library to nearest building			

2. Explain how you used your map to predict the distances.

3. Which one of your buildings is nearest to the library?

4. Now, look at your tiny TIMS Town, and measure the actual distances (as the crow flies) between the buildings. Put your measured distances in the column labeled "Actual Distance in TIMS Town."

5. How close were your predicted and actual distances? In the last column, enter the error (the difference between the predicted distance and the actual distance).

Discuss these questions with your class.

6. What makes a prediction good? Does it have to be exactly right? How close is good enough?

7. If you moved Mr. Origin 4 centimeters to his right, would your data be the same?

Homework

1. Make a data table like this one on your paper. Fill in your data table with the coordinates of the diamond, X, and circle.

Object	Right (in cm)	Front (in cm)
◆		
✖		
●		

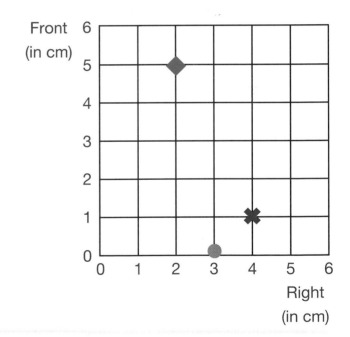

Here is a map Professor Peabody made of his yard. He marked the location of his maple tree with an "M," the location of his oak tree with an "O," and the location of his poplar tree with a "P." He also drew a circle showing where his rose garden is.

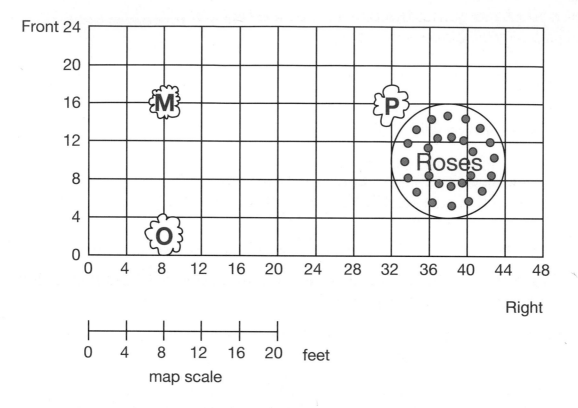

2. How far is it from the maple tree to the poplar tree? Tell how you know.

3. How wide is the rose garden?

4. How far is it from the maple tree to the oak tree? Tell how you know.

5. What is the distance between the poplar tree and the oak tree?

6. Professor Peabody wants to plant an apple tree halfway between the maple tree and the poplar tree. What should the apple tree's coordinates be?

Mapping a Tiny TIMS Town

Tens Game

The object of this game is to make a ten by adding or subtracting the numbers on the cards. Whenever a player makes a ten, he or she adds it to his or her pile. At the end of the game, the player with the biggest pile wins. Two to four players can play.

Materials

- A set of cards with two each of the numbers 1 to 18.

  or

- A set of regular playing cards. Use an ace as 1, a jack as 11, a queen as 12, and a king as 13. You will not use the numbers 14 through 18.

Directions

1. The dealer gives two cards to each player and puts the rest of the cards face down in a stack.

2. Before play begins, each player chooses one card from his or her hand and places it face up on the table.

3. The player to the left of the dealer draws one card from the deck. The player tries to make a ten by adding or subtracting the numbers on any two cards. He can use the two cards in his hand or two of the cards that are face up on the table. He could also use one card from his hand and one of the cards that are face up on the table.

   - If the player can make a ten, he says a number sentence for the cards. (If he has a ten card in his hand, he can make a ten with that ten card alone.) Then, he puts them face down in a pile in front of him. His turn ends.

- If the player cannot make a ten, he must put a card face up in front of him. His turn ends.

When his turn ends, the player draws a card or cards from the deck until he has two cards in his hand. He should also make sure he has at least one card face up on the table.

4. Each player continues like the first player.

5. The game continues until all the cards in the deck are gone, and no player can make another ten. Whoever has the most cards in his or her face-down pile at the end of the game is the winner.

Challenge

Play this game using the same rules, except make a different number. For example, you may try to make 11, instead of 10.

Another variation is to allow players to use more than two cards to make a ten. For example, 5 + 3 + 2.

You may decide to change the rules. For example, if a player makes a ten, he gets another turn.

Homework

Dear Family Member:

Playing this game is a good way to practice the addition and subtraction facts. Help your child learn these facts by playing the game with him or her.

Thank you for your cooperation.

Teach a family member to play this game. Mark down how many minutes you play. Also, record the number sentences that you created while playing.

Tall Buildings

This is a review of things you learned earlier.

Building	City	Height (in feet)
John Hancock Tower	Chicago	1127
Sears Tower	Chicago	1454
Space Needle	Seattle	605
Empire State Building	New York	1250

Use the data in the table to help you solve the problems below. Show how you solved each problem.

1. Write down the heights of the buildings in order from smallest to largest.

2. How many feet taller is the Sears Tower than the John Hancock Tower?

3. **A.** A three-story school building is about 50 feet tall. About how many times taller is the Space Needle?

   B. About how many times taller is the Sears Tower?

4. About how many times taller is the Empire State Building than the Space Needle?

5. The CN Tower in Toronto, Canada, is 361 feet taller than the Sears Tower. How tall is the CN Tower?

6. **A.** The Petronas Tower in Kuala, Malaysia, is 332 feet shorter than the CN Tower. How tall is Petronas Tower?

   B. Is the Petronas Tower taller or shorter than the Sears Tower? By how many feet?

7. Solve the following problems. Estimate to be sure your answers are reasonable. Explain your estimation strategies.

   A. 7234
        + 3849

   B. 632
        − 485

Unit 9

USING PATTERNS TO PREDICT

	Student Guide	Discovery Assignment Book	Adventure Book	Unit Resource Guide*
Lesson 1				
Measuring Mass	◎			◎
Lesson 2				
Mass vs. Number	◎	◎		◎
Lesson 3				
More Mass Problems	◎			

Unit Resource Guide pages are from the teacher materials.

Measuring Mass

What is mass?

Mass is the amount of matter in an object. We can get an idea about the mass of an object by lifting it up.

If we want to compare the mass of two things, we can use a two-pan balance. But before we use the balance, we make sure it is leveled. You can use a small piece of clay to level your balance by placing it on the side that is higher.

In order to measure mass, we need a unit of measure. Common metric units of mass are the **gram** (g) and the **kilogram** (kg). A kilogram is 1000 grams. So, we measure the mass of small objects in grams and the mass of large objects in kilograms. The mass of a centimeter connecting cube is one gram. The mass of a third grader is about 25–40 kilograms.

We can find the mass of an object using the two-pan balance.

Leon used his two-pan balance to find the mass of his calculator. His standard masses have a mass of 1 gram and 10 grams. He found the mass was 92 grams. Can you see why?

Use a two-pan balance to find the mass of at least four objects your teacher provides. Record your results in a data table like the one below.

O Object	M Mass (in _____) *unit*

Use your data to answer the following questions. Sometimes, you will have to collect more data to provide an answer.

1. Which object had the most mass?

2. Which object had the least mass?

3. Choose any two of your objects, and use your data to predict the total mass of those two objects together.

   A. Write down the mass of each object and your prediction.

   B. Use the balance to find the actual mass of the two objects together.

   C. Was your predicted mass close to the actual mass? How close?

4. A. Put the object with the most mass in one pan. Put the object with the second largest mass in the other pan. Predict how much mass you will have to add to the lighter side to get the pans to balance, and write down your prediction.

   B. Check your prediction by adding mass to the lighter side until the pans balance. Write down the actual amount. Are the two numbers close?

5. Compare the mass of the objects from Questions 1 and 2. Describe how the masses compare, using words or number sentences.

6. Were any of your predictions different from your actual results? Discuss why that might have happened.

7. All the groups in your class found the mass of at least one identical object. Did everyone get the same measurement for its mass? Were all the measurements close? Discuss why the answers were not exactly the same.

Homework

Dear Family Member:

Your child is learning about mass, the amount of matter in an object, in class. As homework, your child will find the number of grams of mass in various food packages. If there are not enough items in your home, take your child with you to the supermarket. Your child should record the information he or she gathers in a two-column data table like the one on these pages.

Thank you for your cooperation.

Look at the labels on some food containers at home or in the store. Find the mass of the contents in grams. Put your data in a table like the one below.

B Brand Name	M Mass (in g)
100% Bran cereal	482
Chunk White Tuna	173

1. What is the largest mass you found?

2. What is the smallest mass you found?

3. Which two things' masses are closest together? How did you figure this out?

4. Make a new data table with your items in order from lightest to heaviest.

Mass vs. Number

Yolanda bakes wonderful oat bran bars. Since her friends like the bars so much, she decided to start her own business selling them. When customers send her an order, she will ship the oat bran bars to them through the mail. The mailing cost depends on the mass of each package. Since her customers will order different numbers of bars, she will need to know the mass of different numbers of bars so that she can purchase her stamps ahead of time.

Yolanda finds that the mass of one oat bran bar is 18 grams. Here is the data that Yolanda recorded when she measured the mass of the oat bran bars.

N Number of Oat Bran Bars	M Mass (in g)
1	18
2	39
4	71
6	110

Yolanda made a graph of her data.

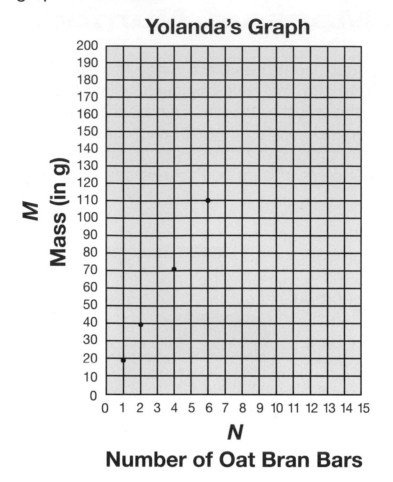

Yolanda's Graph

M **Mass (in g)**

N
Number of Oat Bran Bars

"I see a pattern," she said. "It looks like the data points are on a straight line." So, Yolanda tried to draw a straight line through her data points. She could not get a line to go through all the points, but she tried to fit the points as best she could. Scientists call that a **best-fit line.**

"Well," says Yolanda, "I know the mass of one, two, four, and six bars. So, I should be able to predict the mass of any number of bars." How can she predict the mass of three bars?

We will carry out an investigation called *Mass vs. Number* to see if we get the same kind of pattern as Yolanda. You will be finding the mass of a number of objects your teacher gives you. Later, you can use this information to help Yolanda find the weight of her oat bran bar packages.

Paul and Michael's Pencils

1. Paul and Michael did the experiment with these pencils.

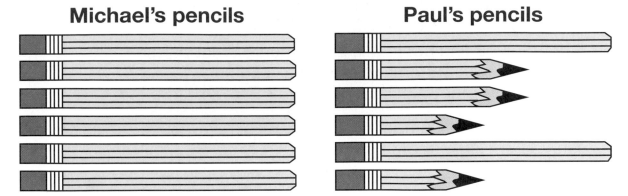

Michael's pencils　　　　　　　　　**Paul's pencils**

A. Which data table below is Paul's and which is Michael's? Explain.

Mass vs. Number

N Number of Pencils	M Mass (in g)
1	11
2	22
3	33
4	44
6	66

Mass vs. Number

N Number of Pencils	M Mass (in g)
1	11
2	19
3	26
4	31
6	46

B. Which graph looks like Paul's and which looks like Michael's?
Explain how you know.

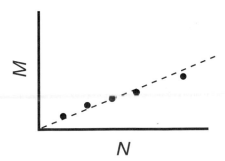

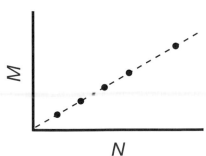

2. What did you find out in this experiment? What patterns did you find? Compare these patterns to the ones in *Lemonade Stand* in Unit 7 Lesson 1. Are they similar or different? Explain.

3. If you double the number of objects, what happens to the mass? How can you check your prediction?

4. If you triple the number of objects, what happens to the mass? Explain how you found your answer.

5. If you increase the number of objects by 2, does the mass go up by 2 grams? Explain.

6. If you extend your line back toward $N = 0$, what value for the mass (M) do you get? Does this seem reasonable? Why or why not?

Homework

Yolanda's Oat Bran Bars

Orders for Yolanda's oat bran bars have arrived! Yolanda needs to use her best-fit line to make predictions. Does Yolanda have enough data to find the mass of each order?

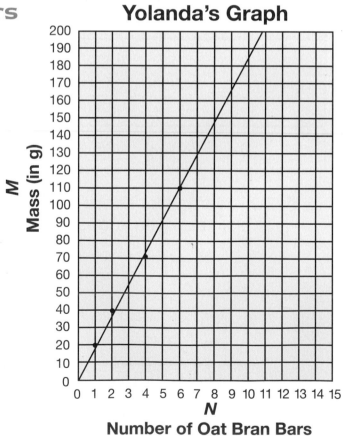

Can you make some predictions from Yolanda's best-fit line? Use her best-fit line to complete a data table like the one below.

N Number of Oat Bran Bars	M Mass (in g)
1	18
2	39
3	
4	71
5	
6	110
8	
12	
	200

More Mass Problems

1. Professor Peabody did an investigation like *Mass vs. Number* using some wooden spheres. Oops, he spilled some paint on his data table! Can you estimate what the missing numbers were? Make your best estimate for the blanks.

N Number of Spheres	M Mass (in g)
4	30
	61
12	

2. In the data table for Question 1, did the mass double when you doubled the number of spheres? Explain.

3. Here are some objects. Next to each object, we have written different masses. Choose the mass that is most likely to be accurate for each object.

Pencil	2 g	10 g	100 g	200 g
Ham Sandwich	2 g	10 g	100 g	200 g
Penny	2 g	10 g	100 g	200 g

4. Tiffany did an investigation like *Mass vs. Number* with pieces of chalk. Here is her graph.

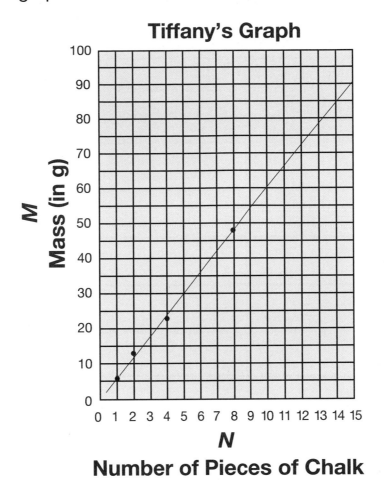

Tiffany's Graph

M — Mass (in g)

N
Number of Pieces of Chalk

A. What is the mass of ten pieces of chalk?

B. If she kept adding chalk until she had a mass of about 70 g, about how many pieces of chalk would there be in the pan? Would their mass be exactly 70 g? Explain.

C. Predict the mass of 30 pieces of chalk. Explain how you found your answer.

5. Bill was packing marbles into a box. He wanted to know what the box would weigh after he finished. Each of his marbles has a mass of exactly 6 grams, and the box has a mass of 50 grams. Make a complete data table, including values for the missing numbers.

N Number of Marbles	M Mass of Box and Marbles (in g)
0	
1	56
2	
3	68
4	
8	
	110

6. On a sheet of graph paper, make a graph of the marble and box data in Question 5. Number your axes so you have enough room for the values $M = 110$ g and $N = 30$ marbles.

7. Which of the following graphs looks most like your graph? Explain why it looks like your graph.

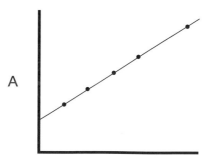

A

More Mass Problems

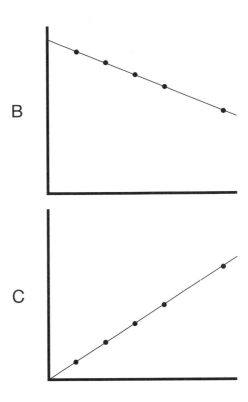

Metric Fun

8. Estimate your weight in kilograms by dividing your weight in pounds by 2.

9. Decide whether the following statements "could be" true or if they are "crazy." If the statement is crazy, tell what each student might have done wrong and correct the statement.

   A. Samantha weighs 80 pounds. She said that her weight in kilograms is about 160 kilograms.

   B. Byron found his weight in kilograms. It was 32 kilograms. He said his weight in pounds is about 64 pounds.

   C. Ashley found the weight of her bird. It weighs half a pound. She said that her bird's weight in kilograms is about one-quarter of a kilogram.

   D. Natalie's baby sister, Jessica, weighs 13 pounds. She said that Jessica's weight in kilograms is about 30 kilograms.

   E. Marissa's new puppy weighs 16 kilograms. She said that her puppy's weight in pounds is about 10 pounds.

Unit 10

Numbers and Patterns: An Assessment Unit

	Student Guide	Discovery Assignment Book	Adventure Book	Unit Resource Guide*
Lesson 1				
Stencilrama	@	@		
Lesson 2				
Problem Game	@	@		
Lesson 3				
Class Party				@
Lesson 4				
Word Problems for Review	@			
Lesson 5				
Midyear Test				@

Unit Resource Guide pages are from the teacher materials.

Stencilrama

The children in Mrs. Cho's class decorated the room with geometric designs from cultures around the world. Look at the picture of the room on page 128. Students made borders to decorate different places in the room by repeating designs over and over again on long pieces of paper.

To be able to repeat the same design exactly, students made stencils. Here is the way Liz and Jody made theirs.

- They looked through a book of African designs and found a design they liked on a piece of cloth from Nigeria.

- Liz and Jody drew the design on a card.

- They cut the design out of the card and used the card as their stencil.

- The girls decided to take turns coloring the design on the border.

- Liz placed the stencil at the edge of a long piece of paper and used markers to color in the cut-out space. She made a mark at the edge of the stencil so Jody would know where to place the stencil on her turn.

- When Jody took her turn coloring the design, she decided to make the design more interesting by turning the card upside down. She was careful to place the short side of the stencil across the top of the border, just as Liz did.

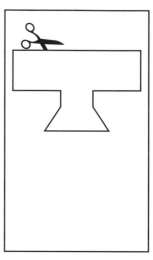

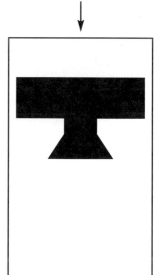

This is the way the border looked after they used the stencil three times.

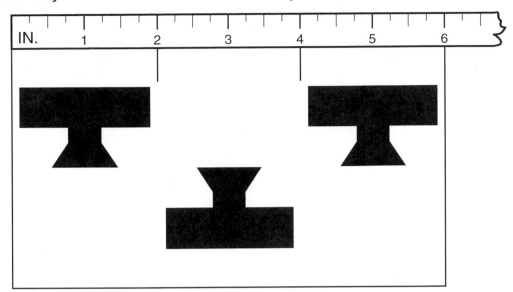

Since the class wanted to make borders of different lengths, they decided to investigate how the number of times they used the stencil affected the length of the border. Students collected data and made data tables. Here is Liz and Jody's data table.

N Number of Stencils	L Length of Border (in inches)
1	2 inches
2	4 inches
4	8 inches

This data table reminded students of the data table they made for *Lemonade Stand*. They remembered how they used a graph of that data to make predictions about the number of lemons in a pitcher of lemonade.

So, the girls decided to make a graph of their stencil data. They used the graph to predict the number of stencils they needed for a border the length of Mrs. Cho's desk.

If your class decided to decorate your classroom using borders made with stencils, you would need to solve some problems. Here are some questions to discuss about Liz and Jody's data.

1. What variables did Liz and Jody compare in their data table?

2. What stayed the same as they made their borders?

3. What did Liz and Jody do to collect the data that they wrote in their data table?

4. What would Liz and Jody need to know to find the number of times they will use the stencil to make a border across the top of the blackboard?

Some Designs from Cultures of the World

Below are designs found on objects from different cultures. Also included is one type of stencil you might make from the design.

I.

Design adapted from the Hmong People of Laos

Stencil adapted from design

Border made from stencil

2.

Design adapted from an Iroquois
wampum belt

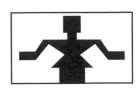

Stencil adapted from design

3.

Design adapted from a Navaho blanket

Stencil adapted from design

4.

Design adapted from Musuyidie,
a West African symbol

Stencil adapted from design

5.

Design adapted from a South American beaded apron

Stencil adapted from design

6.

Design adapted from a Lithuanian candleholder

Stencil adapted from design

7.

Design adapted from a wooden box made in the Democratic Republic of Congo, formerly Zaire

Stencil adapted from design

Problem Game

Here are instructions for the *Problem Game* for two or more players.

You will need:

- *Problem Game* game board
- *Subtraction Flash Cards for Groups 1–8*
- scratch paper for writing answers
- a clear spinner or a paper clip and a pencil
- a token for each player

1. Put the spinner over the spinner base on the *Problem Game Spinner* Game Page from the *Discovery Assignment Book*. (Or use a pencil and paper clip as a spinner.)

2. Put the flash cards, problem side up, on the Problem Cards rectangle.

3. Each player puts his or her token in the Start rectangle.

4. Spin to see who goes first.

5. When it is your turn, solve the top problem on the Problem Card stack. Say the answer aloud. If you are wrong, then your turn is over.

6. If you are right, spin the spinner, and move that many spaces.

7. Follow any directions written on the space you land on. Sometimes, arrows help you move forward or make you go back.

8. Put the Problem Card on the Discard rectangle.

9. The first player to reach the Finish rectangle (or beyond) is the winner.

This game can be used with different card sets. Your teacher will help you choose the type of problems you will solve each time you play.

Word Problems for Review

1. Find the area of the following shape.

1 sq cm = ☐

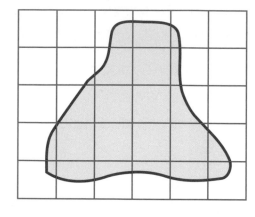

2. Lake Superior's deepest point is 1333 ft. Lake Michigan's deepest point is 923 ft. How much deeper is Lake Superior than Lake Michigan at these points?

3. Fill in the table to give the location of the four shapes.

Object	Right	Front
●		
▲		
■		
♥		

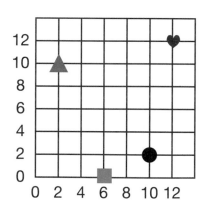

4. The Mississippi River is 2348 miles long, the Missouri River is 2315 miles long, the Rio Grande is 1885 miles long, and the Arkansas River is 1396 miles long. Put these four numbers in order from smallest to largest.

5. Michael ran 1157 feet before he stopped to rest. He then ran another 798 feet. What is the total distance he ran?

6. 4 × 8 = ? Write a story and draw a picture about 4 × 8. Write a number sentence on your picture.

7. How many meters is it from the door of the school building to the playground? Explain how you found your answer.

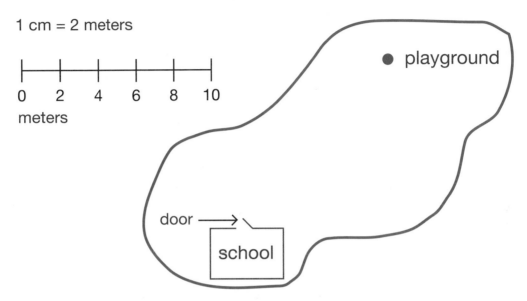

1 cm = 2 meters

0 2 4 6 8 10
meters

playground

door →

school

8. **A.** Predict the 4 missing numbers for this Mass vs. Number data.

N Number of Crayons	M Mass (g)
2	28
4	
	84
8	
	140

B. Predict the mass of one crayon.
C. Predict the mass of five crayons.
D. Predict the mass of 20 crayons.

Unit 11
MULTIPLICATION PATTERNS

	Student Guide	Discovery Assignment Book	Adventure Book	Unit Resource Guide*
Lesson 1				
Lizardland Problems	◎			
Lesson 2				
Handy Facts		◎		
Lesson 3				
Multiplication and Rectangles	◎			
Lesson 4				
Completing the Table	◎	◎		
Lesson 5				
Floor Tiler		◎		
Lesson 6				
Division in Lizardland	◎			
Lesson 7				
Cipher Force!			◎	
Lesson 8				
Multiples of Tens and Hundreds	◎	◎		

Unit Resource Guide pages are from the teacher materials.

Lizardland Problems

To solve these problems, look for clues in the picture of Lizardland on the previous pages. Write about how you solved each problem. Use number sentences, pictures, or words.

1. Mr. Brown bought ice cream for his five children at the stand near Picnic Park. How much did he spend?

2. How many blocks are in the wall, including the blocks that are under the signs?

3. Each block in the front wall is 8 inches high.
   A. How high is the wall?
   B. Could you climb over it?
   C. Could you jump over it?
   D. Explain.

4. George has been watching the Lizard-Go-Round. It takes 30 seconds to go around one time.
   A. How many minutes does it take to go around eight times?
   B. How many times does it go around in $2\frac{1}{2}$ minutes?

5. Write a problem about Lizardland, and solve it using multiplication.

Homework

Refreshments

1. Tom is at the refreshment stand with his parents. They are buying three hot dogs, two fries, two lemonades, and one milk. How much will their order cost?

Buying Balloons

2. Mary's mother bought one balloon for Mary and one for Louise. How much did she pay?

3. José is near the Lizard Kingdom. How much did his balloons cost?

The Skyway

4. Joel wants to ride the Skyway. He is the one in line who is wearing the big hat and sunglasses. He noticed that a new car is loaded every 2 minutes. How long will he have to wait after the car that is now being loaded leaves?

The Lizard Show

5. Seats for today's Lizard Show are selling fast. So far, $400 has been collected. How many seats are left? Show your work with number sentences.

Leaping Lizard Roller Coaster

6. How many people can ride in all eight cars of the roller coaster at one time?

7. Jean wants to ride the roller coaster. There are 24 people in front of Jean. She is the one at the end of the line. Will there be enough room for her the next time it is loaded, or will she have to wait?

Ticket Sales

8. The Moore family—Grandmother Moore, Mr. and Mrs. Moore, and the three Moore children—is eating lunch beside Lizard Lake. It is Saturday. How much did they spend on admission tickets for the carnival? (Hint: The admission ticket price is beside the ticket taker at the front gate.)

9. How much would the Moores have saved on admission if they had come on Tuesday?

Multiplication and Rectangles

I made a rectangle with 8 tiles. My sentence is $4 \times 2 = 8$ since there are 4 rows of 2 tiles each.

I made this rectangle with 8 tiles. I wrote $1 \times 8 = 8$ since there is 1 row of 8 tiles.

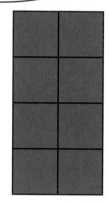

I put these 6 tiles in 2 rows of 3 tiles, so $6 = 2 \times 3$.

That means that 2 and 3 are **factors** of six. Are there any other factors of six?

Exploring Factors of 6 Using Tiles

1. Arrange 6 square tiles into rectangles in as many ways as you can.

2. Draw your rectangles on *Centimeter Grid Paper.*

3. Write multiplication sentences inside each rectangle.

Exploring Factors of 12 and 18 Using Tiles

4. Arrange 12 tiles into rectangles in as many ways as you can. Then, draw your rectangles on graph paper, and write multiplication sentences inside each rectangle.

5. Do the same thing with 18 tiles.

Exploring Factors of 5 and 7 Using Tiles

6. Arrange 5 and 7 tiles into rectangles in as many ways as you can.

7. How are the rectangles you can make for 5 and 7 different from the ones you can make for 6, 12, and 18?

Exploring Turn-around Facts

8. Choose a multiplication fact, and turn its factors around. For example,

   $2 \times 3 = 6$ can be turned around to make $3 \times 2 = $ _____ . Make a rectangle to match your new fact.

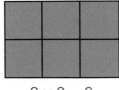

$2 \times 3 = 6$

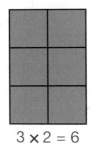

$3 \times 2 = 6$

9. We call the facts that we get from old ones in this way **turn-around facts.** Record in your multiplication table all facts that are turn-around facts for the ones you've already recorded.

Exploring Square Numbers

10. Use your tiles to build squares of different sizes, up to at least 10 × 10. Count the number of tiles on each side and the total number of tiles in each square. Make a table like this one.

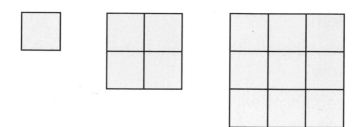

Number on a Side	Number in Square	Multiplication Facts
1	1	1 × 1 = 1
2	4	2 × 2 = 4
3	9	

11. The numbers 1, 4, 9, and so on are called **square numbers.** Enter your facts from Question 10 about square numbers in your multiplication table.

12. Do you see a pattern for square numbers?

Homework

Tile Problems

Use tiles to help you solve these problems. Write a number sentence to go with each problem.

1. Sam made a rectangle with 30 tiles. If there were 6 rows, how many were in each row?

2. Julia made a rectangle with 7 rows and 5 in each row. How many tiles did she use?

3. Sara made an array with 24 tiles. There were 8 tiles in each row. How many rows were there?

4. A rectangle of 12 tiles has tiles of 3 different colors. There is an equal number of tiles of each color. How many tiles of each color are there?

5. Arrange 20 tiles into rectangles in as many ways as you can. Write a number sentence for each rectangle.

6. Arrange 11 tiles into rectangles in as many ways as you can. Write a number sentence for each rectangle.

Multiplication and Rectangles

Completing the Table

You should have only 20 blank squares left in your multiplication table. Use any strategy you like—skip counting, a calculator, a number line, or counters—to find the remaining facts.

When you find a fact, such as 4×6, you can also record its turn-around fact—in this case, 6×4.

Patterns for Nine

1. Copy and complete the list of facts for 9. Then, write the products in a column, one on each line.

   $0 \times 9 = ?$

   $1 \times 9 = ?$

   $2 \times 9 = ?$

   $3 \times 9 = ?$

   $4 \times 9 = ?$

   $5 \times 9 = ?$

   $6 \times 9 = ?$

   $7 \times 9 = ?$

   $8 \times 9 = ?$

   $9 \times 9 = ?$

2. What patterns do you see in your list?

3. Use your calculator to find the products below. Then, add the digits in each product. Repeat adding the digits until you get a one digit number.

Example: $9 \times 634 = 5706$ $5 + 7 + 0 + 6 = 18$ $1 + 8 = 9$

A. 9×47

B. 9×83

C. 9×89

D. 9×92

E. 9×123

F. 9×633

G. 9×697

H. 9×333

4. Describe what happens when you add the digits of a multiple of 9.

Multiplication Facts and Triangle Flash Cards

With a partner, use the directions below and your *Triangle Flash Cards: 5s* and *Triangle Flash Cards: 10s* to practice the multiplication facts.

- One partner covers the shaded number, the largest number on the card. This number will be the answer to the multiplication problem. It is called the **product.**

$5 \times 4 = ?$

$4 \times 5 = ?$

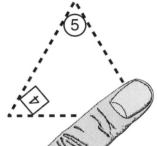

- The second person multiplies the two uncovered numbers (one in a circle, one in a square). These are the two **factors.** It doesn't matter which of the factors is said first. 4×5 and 5×4 both equal 20.

- Separate the facts into three piles: those facts you know and can answer quickly, those that you can figure out with a strategy, and those that you need to learn.

- Discuss how you can figure out facts that you do not recall right away. Share your strategies with your partner.

- Practice the last two piles again and then make a list of the facts you need to practice at home for homework.

- Circle the facts you know quickly on your *Multiplication Facts I Know* chart. Remember that if you know one fact, you also know its turn-around fact. Circle both on your chart.

Multiplication Facts I Know

×	0	1	2	3	4	5	6	7	8	9	10
0	0	0	0	0	0	0	0	0	0	0	0
1	0	1	2	3	4	5	6	7	8	9	10
2	0	2	4	6	8	10	12	14	16	18	20
3	0	3	6	9	12	15	18	21	24	27	30
4	0	4	8	12	16	(20)	24	28	32	36	40
5	0	5	10	15	(20)	25	30	35	40	45	50
6	0	6	12	18	24	30	36	42	48	54	60
7	0	7	14	21	28	35	42	49	56	63	70
8	0	8	16	24	32	40	48	56	64	72	80
9	0	9	18	27	36	45	54	63	72	81	90
10	0	10	20	30	40	50	60	70	80	90	100

Homework

Find these products.

1. $3 \times 4 = ?$

2. $6 \times 7 = ?$

3. $6 \times 5 = ?$

4. $5 \times 4 = ?$

5. $7 \times 9 = ?$

6. $4 \times 2 = ?$

7. $8 \times 5 = ?$

8. $8 \times 8 = ?$

9. $7 \times 4 = ?$

10. $0 \times 6 = ?$

11. $7 \times 3 = ?$

12. $9 \times 6 = ?$

13. $6 \times 8 = ?$

14. $7 \times 8 = ?$

15. $9 \times 9 = ?$

16. $\begin{array}{r} 7 \\ \times\,5 \\ \hline \end{array}$

17. $\begin{array}{r} 6 \\ \times\,9 \\ \hline \end{array}$

18. $\begin{array}{r} 3 \\ \times\,8 \\ \hline \end{array}$

19. $\begin{array}{r} 4 \\ \times\,6 \\ \hline \end{array}$

20. $\begin{array}{r} 8 \\ \times\,3 \\ \hline \end{array}$

21. $\begin{array}{r} 9 \\ \times\,1 \\ \hline \end{array}$

22. $\begin{array}{r} 8 \\ \times\,4 \\ \hline \end{array}$

23. $\begin{array}{r} 6 \\ \times\,6 \\ \hline \end{array}$

24. $\begin{array}{r} 7 \\ \times\,7 \\ \hline \end{array}$

25. Choose one of the facts in Questions 1–24, and write a multiplication story about it. Draw a picture to go with your story.

Division in Lizardland

Look at the picture of Lizardland to help you solve the following problems. Write number sentences to show the answers.

The Brownies

1. There are 21 Brownies and 3 leaders near Picnic Park. To make sure no one gets lost, the leaders split the troop into three smaller groups, each with its own adult leader. Each group is the same size. How many Brownies are in each group?

2. The 21 Brownies and their 3 leaders rode the Leaping Lizard Roller Coaster. How many cars on the roller coaster did they fill?

3. Each table in Picnic Park can seat eight people. Are there enough empty tables for the Brownies and their leaders?

The Moore Family

4. The Moore family is having a picnic by Lizard Lake. Mrs. Moore brought three large oranges to be shared among her family of six. How much will each person get? Write a division sentence for your answer.

5. Mrs. Moore brought six cookies to be shared among her 3 children. How many cookies will each child get? Write a division sentence for your answer. Compare your number sentence with the one you got for Question 4.

Division in Lizardland

Zero

6. Mr. Moore baked some cupcakes for his family to share. Unfortunately, he didn't remember to bring them, so he had zero cupcakes to share among six people. Use this story to write about the value of $0 \div 6$.

7. The ticket taker has 100 game tokens to give to the first several families who enter the park.

   A. If he gives 4 game tokens to each family that enters the park, how many families will get four tokens before he runs out? If he gives 2 game tokens to each family, how many families will enter before he runs out? How many families will get a token if he gives 1 token to each family? Be sure to write number sentences to show your answers.

   B. If he gives 0 tokens to each family, how many families will enter the park before he runs out of tokens? Use this story to tell about the value of $100 \div 0$.

Fact Families

Multiplication and division facts are related. Questions 8–10 will show you what they have in common. The four facts in each question make up a **fact family.**

8. A. $4 \times 5 = ?$
   B. $5 \times 4 = ?$
   C. $20 \div 5 = ?$
   D. $20 \div 4 = ?$

9. A. $2 \times 9 = ?$
   B. $9 \times 2 = ?$
   C. $18 \div 2 = ?$
   D. $18 \div 9 = ?$

10. A. $6 \times 8 = ?$
    B. $8 \times 6 = ?$
    C. $48 \div 8 = ?$
    D. $48 \div 6 = ?$

Division Symbols

The symbols in these division sentences mean the same thing:

$$24 \div 6 = 4 \qquad 24/6 = 4 \qquad 6\overline{)24}\,^{4}$$

11. $16/4 = ?$

12. $45 \div 9 = ?$

13. $8\overline{)64}\,^{?}$

14. $5\overline{)40}\,^{?}$

Homework

Related Multiplication and Division Problems

1. **A.** $8 \times 3 = ?$
   B. $24 \div 3 = ?$
   C. $24/8 = ?$
   D. $3 \times 8 = ?$

2. **A.** $6 \times 4 = ?$
   B. $24/4 = ?$
   C. $24 \div 6 = ?$
   D. $4 \times 6 = ?$

3. **A.** $5 \times 8 = ?$
   B. $40 \div 8 = ?$
   C. $5 \overline{)40}$ with $?$ on top
   D. $8 \times 5 = ?$

4. **A.** $9 \times 6 = ?$
   B. $54 \div 6 = ?$
   C. $9 \overline{)54}$ with $?$ on top
   D. $6 \times 9 = ?$

Division Problems

5. $8 \div 2 = ?$

6. $27/3 = ?$

7. $10/1 = ?$

8. $6 \overline{)36}$ with $?$ on top

9. $40 \div 10 = ?$

10. $72/9 = ?$

11. $18/3 = ?$

12. $0 \div 7 = ?$

13. $25 \div 5 = ?$

14. $60/6 = ?$

15. $4 \overline{)12}$ with $?$ on top

16. $3 \overline{)21}$ with $?$ on top

17. Write a division story that fits one of the number sentences in Questions 1–16.

Multiples of Tens and Hundreds

1. What pattern for multiplying a number by ten did you find in the multiplication table? Write two examples that show your pattern.

2. Use the pattern to predict these products. Use a calculator to check your predictions.

   A. $10 \times 24 = ?$ B. $10 \times 37 = ?$

   C. $10 \times 40 = ?$ D. $10 \times 348 = ?$

   E. $100 \times 6 = ?$ F. $100 \times 12 = ?$

   G. $100 \times 34 = ?$ H. $100 \times 876 = ?$

3. Solve the following problems.

   A. $2 \times 3 = ?$ B. $2 \times 30 = ?$ C. $2 \times 300 = ?$

   D. $2 \times 4 = ?$ E. $2 \times 40 = ?$ F. $2 \times 400 = ?$

   G. $3 \times 6 = ?$ H. $3 \times 60 = ?$ I. $3 \times 600 = ?$

   J. $4 \times 3 = ?$ K. $4 \times 30 = ?$ L. $4 \times 300 = ?$

4. Solve the following problems.

   A. $\begin{array}{r} 200 \\ \times\, 5 \\ \hline \end{array}$ B. $\begin{array}{r} 300 \\ \times\, 3 \\ \hline \end{array}$ C. $\begin{array}{r} 600 \\ \times\, 4 \\ \hline \end{array}$

   D. $\begin{array}{r} 500 \\ \times\, 7 \\ \hline \end{array}$ E. $\begin{array}{r} 900 \\ \times\, 5 \\ \hline \end{array}$ F. $\begin{array}{r} 600 \\ \times\, 5 \\ \hline \end{array}$

Unit 12

Dissections

	Student Guide	Discovery Assignment Book	Adventure Book	Unit Resource Guide*
Lesson 1				
Tangrams	@	@		@
Lesson 2				
Building with Triangles	@	@		@
Lesson 3				
Building with Four Triangles	@			@
Lesson 4				
Dissection Puzzles	@	@		
Lesson 5				
Hex		@		
Lesson 6				
Focus on Word Problems	@			

Unit Resource Guide pages are from the teacher materials.

Tangrams

The tangram is an old Chinese puzzle. In it, there are seven pieces called tans:

These tangram pieces can be put together in many ways. Designs made with these pieces are called **tangrams.** Some people like to make tangrams that look like animals or other real things. Usually, all seven tans are used. The only rule is that the pieces must touch without overlapping. You may be able to find a book at your library that shows such tangrams.

Tangram Animals

Fill in the outlines of the duck and cat using fewer than seven tangram pieces for each puzzle.

1.

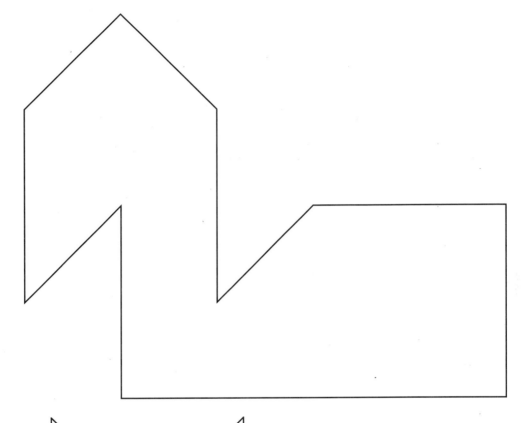

2.

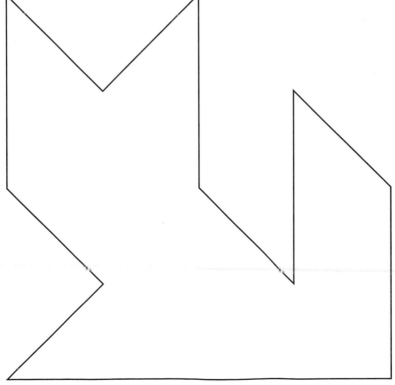

More Tangram Animals

Fill in the outlines of the horse and giraffe using all seven tangram pieces.

3.

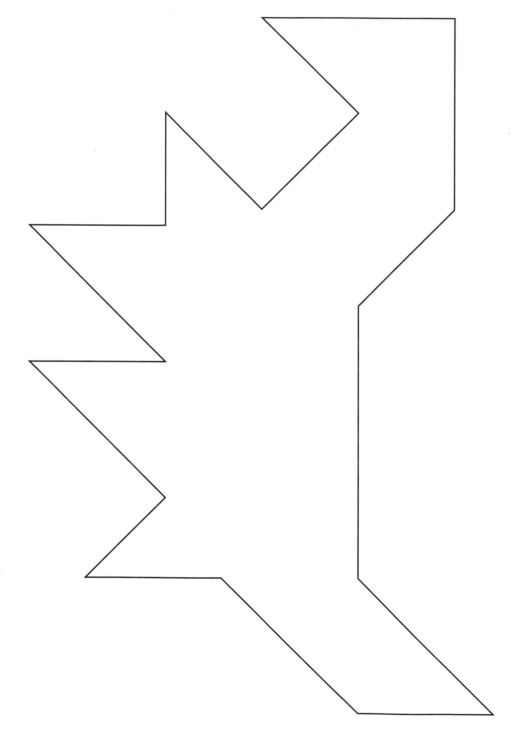

4.

Puzzling Tangrams

Make a square with all seven tangram pieces. With your partner, use the tangram pieces to cover this square completely. Hint: Have the corners of your pieces fall on or very close to the corners of the grid squares.

5.

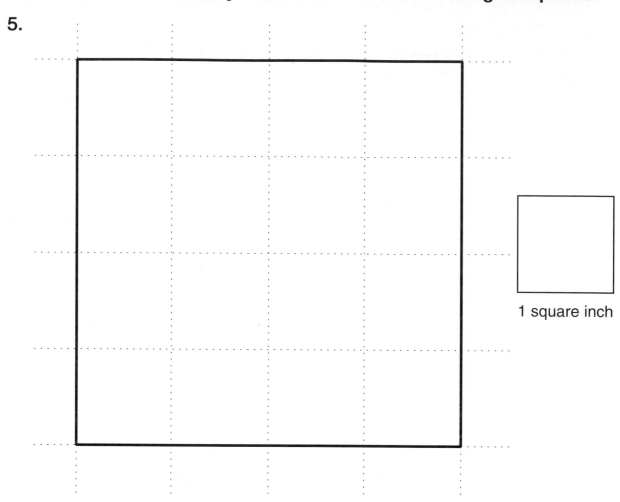

1 square inch

Compare your solution with that of another group.

Try to use all seven pieces to cover each shape in Questions 6–10. Some of the shapes can be covered with the pieces and some cannot. If you cannot cover a shape exactly using all the pieces, explain why. As you try to solve the puzzles, use the questions below to help.

    A. What is the area of the square in Question 5? This is the total area of all your tangram pieces.

    B. What is the area of the shape you are trying to cover?

    C. Can you find a tangram piece to fit in each corner of the shape?

    D. Will you be able to use all the pieces to cover the shape?

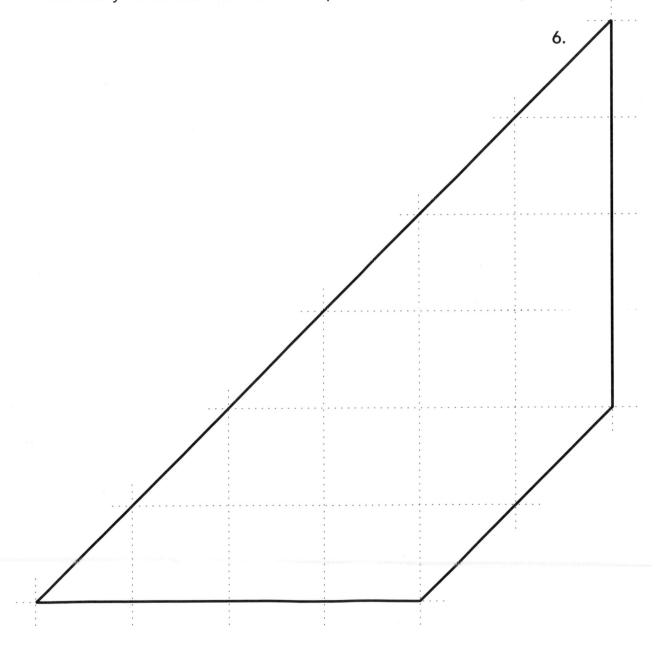

6.

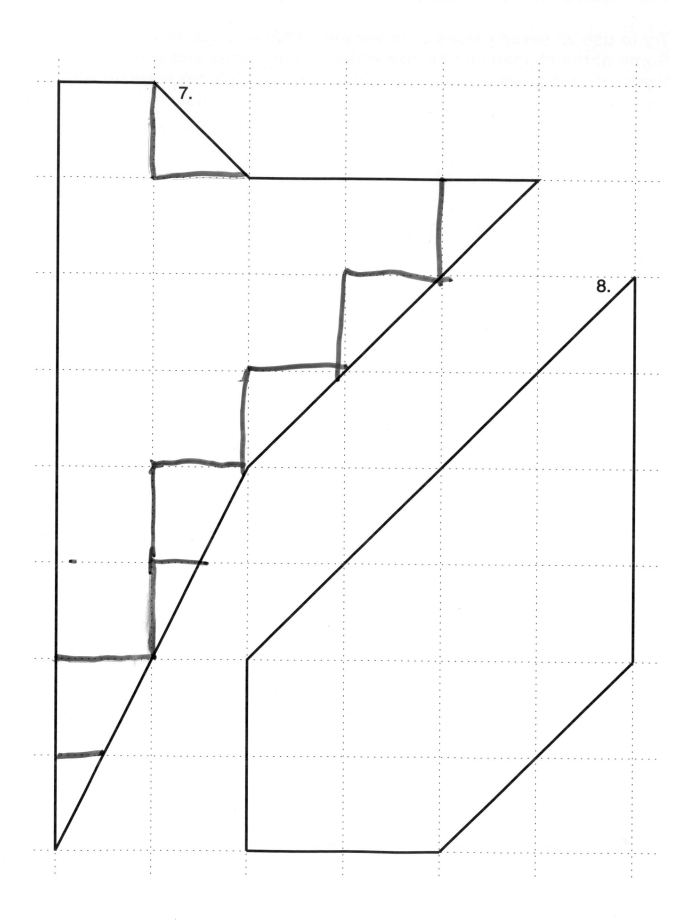

7.

8.

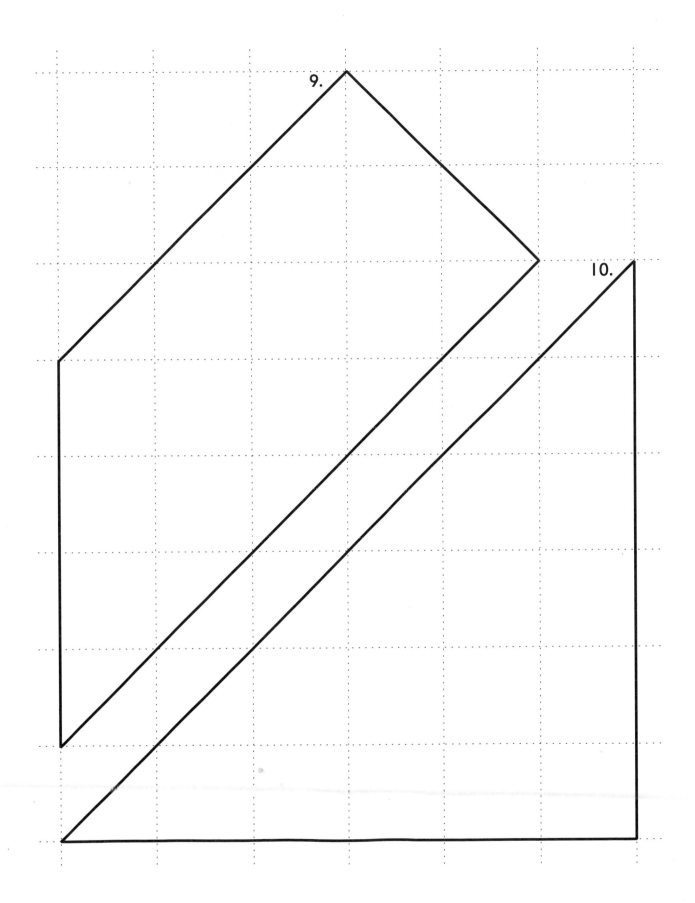

Building with Triangles

You are going to build shapes with triangles like these. First you will build shapes with two triangles, then you will build shapes with three triangles. Many shapes can be made with these triangles. You will learn some geometry as you work with the shapes you make.

Answer the following questions about the triangles shown above.

1. How many sides does each triangle have?

2. In geometry, a corner of a shape is called a **vertex.** (Corners are **vertices.**) How many vertices (corners) does each triangle have?

3. How many **right angles** (square corners) does each of these triangles have? (Hint: To help you decide, you can compare each angle in a triangle with a corner of a square tangram piece.)

4. Measure the area of each triangle to the nearest square inch.

    1 sq in

5. Use a ruler to find the perimeter of each triangle to the nearest half centimeter.

Building with Triangles

There is one rule for building shapes with these triangles. The triangles must be put together edge to edge, like this:

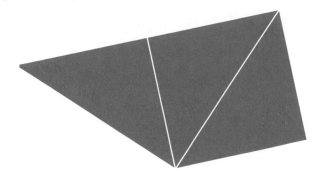

not like this.

We need this rule because otherwise there are too many shapes that can be made.

Building with Two Triangles

To start, you will need two triangles that are the same shape and size as these. You can use triangles from a set of tangrams.

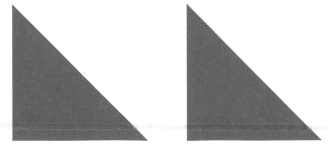

You will also need a ruler, paper and pencil, a marker or crayon, and a data table.

Find all the different shapes you can by putting two triangles together edge to edge. Count two shapes as the same if they are congruent.

Two shapes are **congruent** if they have the same size and shape. You can show that one shape is congruent to another by moving it so that it covers the other shape exactly. You may need to flip it.

Cover one shape below using two triangles. Show that it is congruent to the second shape by moving it to cover the second shape.

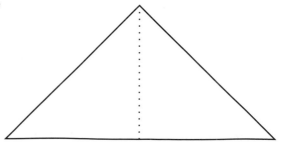

6. Using two triangles, draw all the shapes you find on a sheet of paper. Place dots at the corners and connect the dots with a ruler. Be sure you follow the edge-to-edge rule.

7. Outline the outside border of each shape with a marker or crayon.

8. When you have found all the shapes that can be made with two triangles and have drawn them on a sheet of paper, complete the following for each shape: (Put your answers in a table. Follow the example in the first row of the table.)

   A. Give a name to each shape. Write the name in the first column.

   B. Make a sketch of each shape in the second column of the table.

   C. Count the sides of each shape.

   D. Count the corners (vertices).

   E. Count the right angles inside the shape.

This shape has 3 sides and 1 right angle.

F. Find the area of each shape. (Hint: The area of each small triangle is 1 square inch.)

G. Use a ruler to measure the perimeter of each shape to the nearest half centimeter.

Name of Shape	Sketch	No. of Sides	No. of Corners (vertices)	No. of Right Angles	Area (sq in)	Perimeter (cm)
wing		3	3	1	2	17

9. A. Which of your shapes have line symmetry? (If a shape has **line symmetry,** you can fold the shape in half and the halves will match exactly.)

   B. Draw lines of symmetry on your sketches in the second column of your data table. Follow the example.

10. Find and describe at least one pattern in your table.

Building with Three Triangles

11. Now, find all the shapes that can be made by putting three triangles together edge to edge. Use three triangles like these.

Analyze each of the shapes using Questions 8 and 9 as a guide. Write your answers in a table like the one you used in your work with two triangles.

12. Find and describe a pattern in your new table.

Building with Four Triangles

With four triangles, many shapes can be made.

Here is a **quadrilateral** (a shape with four sides) made from these four pieces. Can you make another four-sided shape with the four triangles?

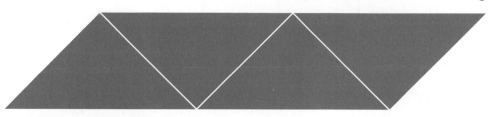

Put four of these triangles together edge to edge to make the shapes listed below. Trace the shapes on paper after you make them (or mark all the corners and use a ruler to connect the marks).

1. a square

2. a rectangle that is not a square

3. a triangle

4. a quadrilateral that is not a rectangle

5. a **pentagon** (a shape with five sides)

6. a **hexagon** (a shape with six sides)

Professor Peabody's Shapes

Professor Peabody made shapes with four triangles put together edge to edge. He used four triangles like this one.

He named his shapes and sketched the outlines, but he forgot to show the inner lines for each triangle.

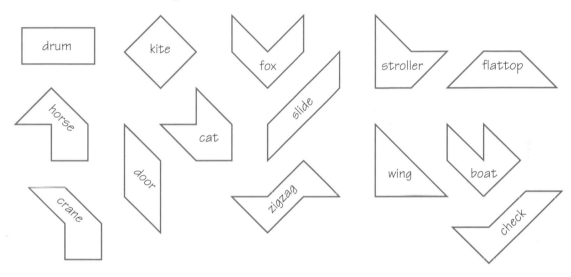

7. Use four triangles to make some of Professor Peabody's shapes. Your teacher will tell you which shapes your group will make and measure. Draw the shapes on paper. Show where the inner triangles go.

8. Count the sides, corners, and right angles for each of the shapes your group is working on. Write this information down next to each shape so you can share it with your classmates.

9. Measure and record the area and perimeter of each shape. Find the perimeter to the nearest half centimeter with your ruler.

Remember we discovered that the area of one small triangle is one square inch.

Be ready to record your measurements in a data table like this one so you can share your data with the class.

Name of Shape	Sketch	No. of Sides	No. of Corners (vertices)	No. of Right Angles	Area (sq in)	Perimeter (cm)

10. Which of Professor Peabody's shapes have line symmetry? Draw the lines of symmetry on your sketches and in the data table.

11. Find and describe a pattern in your data. Explain why the pattern happens.

Professor Peabody's Shape Riddles

Solve Professor Peabody's riddles about his four-triangle shapes.

12. We are the only shapes with 5 sides (pentagons). Who are we?

13. I have the most right angles and the smallest perimeter. Who am I?

14. I have the fewest right angles and the largest perimeter. Who am I?

15. I am a hexagon. If you turn me halfway around, then I look the same. Who am I?

16. I have four lines of symmetry. Who am I?

17. Make up a riddle of your own. The answer to your riddle should be one or more of Professor Peabody's shapes. Use clues about symmetry, area, perimeter, number of sides, and so on. Write your riddle neatly, and write the answer in another place. Trade with a friend and solve each other's riddles. Fix your riddle if it has a mistake.

Dissection Puzzles

Three Triangles

You will need to cut out the pieces for Puzzles A, B, and C on the *Puzzle Pieces* page in the *Discovery Assignment Book.* To answer the questions, you can put the pieces together edge to edge. You can match exactly half of a long edge. You may also need to flip the pieces.

Record your answers for each question on paper by tracing your puzzle pieces.

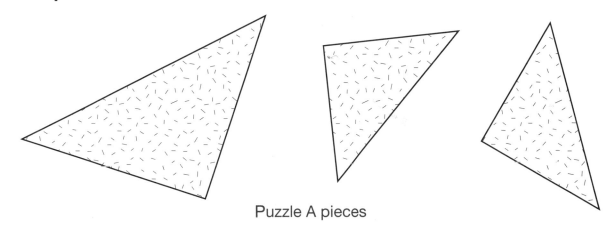

Puzzle A pieces

1. Make a rectangle that is not a square using all three Puzzle A pieces.

2. Make a square using all three Puzzle A pieces.

3. Make a triangle using all three Puzzle A pieces.

Making Squares

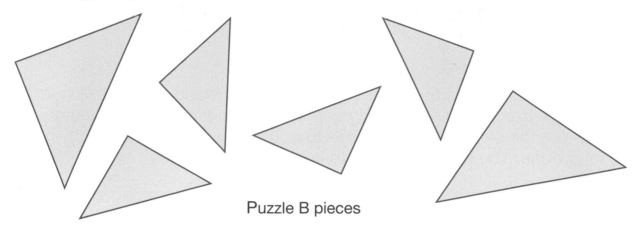

Puzzle B pieces

4. Make three squares using the six Puzzle B pieces.

5. Make two squares using the six Puzzle B pieces.

6. Make one square using the six Puzzle B pieces.

7. Make your own dissection puzzle using the six Puzzle B pieces.
   - Create a design with the Puzzle B pieces.
   - Then, make an outline of your design on paper.
   - On a separate sheet, show where the pieces belong in your design.
   - Trade designs with a friend.

Can you solve each other's puzzles?

Three to Ten Sides

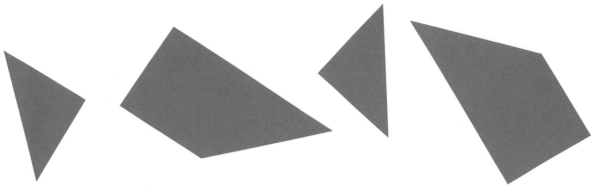

Puzzle C pieces

8. Make a triangle using all four Puzzle C pieces. Remember to use the edge-to-edge rule.

9. Make a quadrilateral (a shape with four sides) using all four Puzzle C pieces.

10. Make a pentagon (a shape with five sides) using all four Puzzle C pieces.

11. Use the Puzzle C pieces to make shapes with six, seven, eight, nine, and ten sides.

Focus on Word Problems

Solve the following problems. Show how you found each answer. You will need a ruler and a copy of *Centimeter Graph Paper* to complete Question 8.

I. One Saturday, 37 people volunteered to help restore a prairie. The team leader wanted to place at least 5 people on each team.

   A. How many teams were there?

   B. How many people were on each team?

2. Mrs. Hix is planning for Girl Scout Camp. Each troop can send 15 members and there are 15 troops coming to camp. About how many Girl Scouts can she expect at camp? Explain your solution.

3. The Girl Scouts are going to Springfield to visit the state capitol. There are 23 girls in the troop. Each car can carry no more than three girls and a driver. How many cars are needed? Explain how you know.

4. Beverly collected 728 pennies. She sorted them into 3 jars. Which jar would you choose if she let you keep one? Explain why you chose that jar.

   A. The first jar had as many pennies as the "2" stands for in 728.

   B. The second jar had as many pennies as the "7" stands for in 728.

   C. The third jar had as many pennies as the "8" stands for in 728.

5. Write a story for this multiplication sentence: $24 \times 3 = ?$

6. Jenny measured the perimeter of a quadrilateral (a shape with four sides). Two sides were 8 centimeters long each. The other two sides were 19 centimeters long. What is the perimeter of the quadrilateral? Write a number sentence to show how you solved the problem.

7. Max found the mass of a box of crayons. He used ten 20-gram masses, five 10-gram masses, one 5-gram mass, and three 1-gram masses. What is the mass of the box of crayons?

8. Caroline loves fruit. She eats four pieces of fruit every day.

   A. Copy her data table on a separate sheet of paper and fill in the missing data.

D Number of Days	F Pieces of Fruit
1	4
2	8
3	
4	

   B. Graph Caroline's data on a piece of *Centimeter Graph Paper.*

   C. How many pieces of fruit will Caroline eat in 9 days? Show how you found your answer on the graph.

9. Mrs. Reynold's class collected aluminum cans for the recycling drive. On Monday they had 436 cans. By Friday they had 712 cans. How many cans did they add to their collection between Monday and Friday?

10. This summer Fred and his father took a road trip. During the first week they traveled 487 miles. During the second week they traveled 346 miles. During their last week they traveled 279 miles.

   A. During the three weeks, estimate if they traveled more or less than 1000 miles.

   B. How many miles did Fred and his father actually drive?

Unit 13

PARTS AND WHOLES

	Student Guide	Discovery Assignment Book	Adventure Book	Unit Resource Guide*
Lesson 1				
Kid Fractions	◉			
Lesson 2				
What's 1?	◉	◉		◉
Lesson 3				
Pizza Problems	◉			◉
Lesson 4				
Fraction Games	◉	◉		
Lesson 5				
Fraction Problems	◉			

Unit Resource Guide pages are from the teacher materials.

Kid Fractions

Mrs. Bond's class is playing *Kid Fractions.* These students are at the front:

Mrs. Bond has written the fraction $\frac{4}{6}$ for a certain part of this group.
The class is trying to guess what Mrs. Bond has in mind.

1. Could Mrs. Bond be thinking of the fraction that are boys?

2. What do you think Mrs. Bond is thinking?

3. Next, Mrs. Bond wrote the fraction $\frac{3}{6}$. Can you guess what she is thinking? Is there a second possibility?

4. Can you think of some other fractions that fit parts of this group? Make a list of fractions for these students. Tell why each fraction fits some part of the group.

Kid Fractions

Homework

Write your answers to the following "family fractions" questions.

1. Draw a picture of the people in your family. Then, write several fractions for parts of your family. Explain each fraction. For example, if you live with your mother and two younger sisters, then you can write $\frac{1}{4}$ for the fraction of your family that is grown up: One of the four people in your family is an adult.

2. Draw a picture of some objects around your house. Then, write several fractions for parts of the group. Explain each fraction. For example, suppose you have five cans of soup, three tomato and two chicken noodle. Then, you could write $\frac{3}{5}$ for the fraction of the cans that are tomato.

3. About what fraction of the utensils (forks, knives, spoons) in your house are forks?

What's 1?

The fraction *one-half* can be big or small, depending on the size of the whole. Half of a personal pizza is not the same as half of an extra-large pizza. Half of a pie for 50¢ is not the same as half a cupcake for 50¢.

You will use pattern blocks to study fractions. In some problems, you are given the fraction and you must find the whole. In others, you are given the whole and you must find the fraction. Both kinds of problems show that to know how big a fraction is, you need to know "What's 1."

You will need a few of each of these pattern blocks.

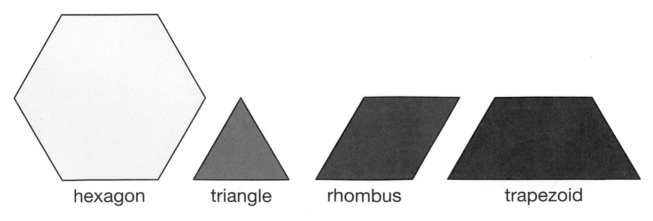

hexagon   triangle   rhombus   trapezoid

Covering Pattern Blocks

1. Look at all your pieces to answer these questions.
   A. How many red pieces cover one yellow?
   B. How many blues cover one yellow?
   C. How many greens cover one yellow?
   D. How many greens cover one blue?
   E. How many greens cover one red?
   F. Use two different colors to cover one red. What did you use?

Wholes to Parts

2. If the yellow hexagon is one whole, then
   A. What piece is one-half?
   B. What piece is one-third?
   C. What piece is one-sixth?
   D. We can write $\frac{2}{6}$ for 2 greens. Write a number for 5 greens.
   E. Write a number for 2 blues.
   F. Write a number for 3 reds.
   G. Write a number for 4 reds.
   H. Is 1 blue more or less than one-half?
   I. Are 2 blues more or less than one-half?

3. This shape is one whole.

   A. How many blues cover the shape?
   B. How many greens cover the shape?
   C. What piece is one-half?
   D. What piece is one-fourth?
   E. Write a fraction for 3 greens.
   F. What other piece makes the same fraction as 3 greens?
   G. Is 1 red more or less than one-half?

Parts to Wholes

4. If the green piece is one-half, what piece is one whole?

5. If the blue is one-third, what is one whole?

6. Trace pattern blocks on a sheet of paper to answer these questions. For example, if the green is 1/3, draw one whole.

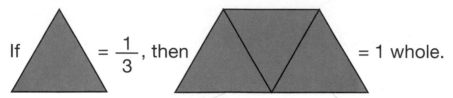

If ⬛ = $\frac{1}{3}$, then ⬛ = 1 whole.

    A. If the green is 1/3, draw 2/3.

    B. If the green is 1/5, draw one whole.

    C. If the red is 1/3, draw one whole.

    D. If the yellow is 1/2, draw one whole.

    E. If the blue is 1/4, draw 3/4.

7. The green shape to the right is one whole.

    A. How many greens cover the shape?

    B. Write a fraction for 1 green.

    C. Write a fraction for 4 greens.

    D. Write a fraction for 7 greens.

    E. Write a fraction for 5 greens.

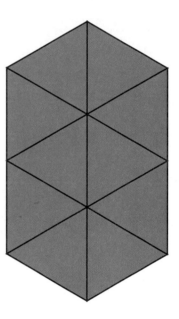

8. The green shape to the right is one whole.

    A. How many blues cover the whole?

    B. Write a fraction for 1 blue.

    C. Write a different fraction for 1 blue.

    D. Write a fraction for 1 red.

    E. Write a fraction for 1 yellow.

    F. Is 1 yellow more or less than one-half?

9. A. If the blue piece is one whole, write a number for 3 greens.

    B. If the blue piece is one whole, write a number for 1 yellow.

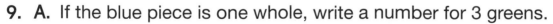

Pizza Problems

Draw pictures and then write words and fractions for your answers to these problems.

1. Mr. Davis is making one pizza for his two daughters, Cora and Felicia. If the two girls share the pizza fairly, then how much will each get?

2. Cora asks if her friend Tanya can stay for dinner, and then Felicia asks if her friend Erin can stay, too. Mr. Davis says both friends can stay. How much pizza will each of the four girls get?

3. Mr. Davis cuts the pizza into eight pieces. How many pieces will each girl get?

4. Just as the girls sit down to eat, Mrs. Davis gets home from work, Tanya's mother rings the doorbell, and Erin's mother calls on the telephone. Now, all four adults also want pizza. If everybody shares one pizza, then what fraction of the pizza will each person get?

5. Suppose your family shared one pizza fairly. What fraction of the pizza would each person get?

For Questions 6–11, it is best to work in a group with four people.
   - **Cut out paper circles to help you find the answers.**
   - **Pretend the circles are pizzas, and share them fairly in your group.**
   - **Draw pictures, and write words and fractions for your answers.**

6. Amber, Alex, Denise, and Jason have a pizza they want to share fairly. How much pizza will each one get?

7. Four people share three pizzas fairly. How much pizza does each person get?

8. Four people share five pizzas fairly. How much does each person get?

9. Four people share six pizzas fairly. How much does each person get?

10. Four people share two and one-half pizzas fairly. How much does each person get?

11. Make up your own number of pizzas to share fairly four ways. How much would each person get?

12. These problems are about sharing five pizzas with more and more people.
    * Copy the table on your own paper.
    * Use paper circles to help you complete the third column.
    * Draw pictures and write words and fractions to show your answers.

Number of People	Number of Pizzas	How much pizza does each person get?
2	5	
4	5	
5	5	
10	5	
20	5	

Homework

Complete these exercises about fractions you can find at home.

1. Vicki drew a picture showing the flavors of yogurt she found in her refrigerator at home.

   A. What fraction of the yogurt is banana? _____

   B. What fraction of the yogurt is cherry? _____

   C. What fraction of the yogurt is strawberry? _____

2. Look for fractions at home and in your neighborhood. You might look in the newspaper (especially in the ads) or in magazines, in cookbooks, in the mail, or on signs. Try to find at least six fractions.

3. Write about each fraction you find. Tell what the whole is, and try to draw a picture that shows the whole and the fraction.

Fraction Games

FractionLand Rules

In this game, a player picks a fraction card and a whole number card. Then, he or she finds the number that is that fraction of the whole number.

Here are instructions for the game *FractionLand* for two or more players.

You will need:
- a token for each player
- a game board
- 1 deck of *FractionLand Whole Number* cards
- 1 deck of *FractionLand Fraction* cards
- 50 connecting cubes, beans, or other counters

1. Shuffle both decks separately. Put them face down next to each other.

2. Put the players' tokens on the Start rectangle.

3. Choose a player to go first.

4. Turn over the top card in each deck. One card shows a fraction and the other, a whole number. Find the fraction of the whole number. Use the counters to help. For example, if you turn up $\frac{1}{2}$ and 12, then divide a group of 12 counters in half. Count the number in each group to find 1/2 of 12. If the answer doesn't come out even (for example, $\frac{1}{4}$ of 9), then you lose your turn.

5. Your answer is the number of squares you can now move forward.

6. Follow any instructions on the square where you land.

7. The first to reach the Finish rectangle (or beyond) is the winner.

Fraction Problem Game Rules

Here are instructions for the *Fraction Problem Game*.

You will need:
- a game board
- problem cards
- scratch paper for writing answers
- a clear spinner or a paper clip and a pencil
- a token for each player
- *Fraction Problem Game Helper* page

1. Put the spinner over the spinner base on the *Problem Game Spinner* Game Page. (Or use a pencil and paper clip as a spinner.)

2. Put the problem cards on the Problem Cards rectangle.

3. Put everyone's token in the Start rectangle.

4. Spin to see who goes first.

5. When it is your turn, take the top card on the Problem Card stack. Compare the two fractions and say a number sentence describing them, using "greater than," "less than," or "equal to." Then, write a number sentence using <, >, or =. If you are wrong, then your turn is over.

6. Use the *Fraction Problem Game Helper* page to help you solve the problems.

7. If you are right, spin the spinner, and move that many spaces.

8. Follow any directions on the space you land on. Sometimes, arrows help you move forward or make you go back.

9. Put the Problem Card on the Discard rectangle.

10. The first player to reach the Finish rectangle (or beyond) is the winner.

This game can be used with different card sets. Your teacher will help you understand what kind of problems you will be solving for each card set.

Fraction Problems

You may use pizza circles, the *Fraction Problem Game Helper* Game Page, counters, a calculator, or drawings to solve these problems. Write your answer to each problem. Be prepared to tell how you solved the problem.

1. Which divisions show fourths? Explain.

A.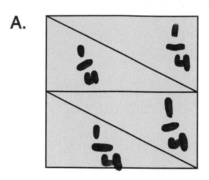

B.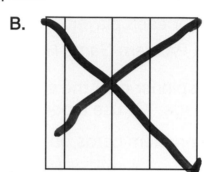

C.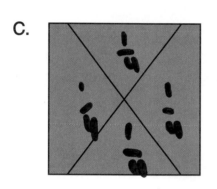

D.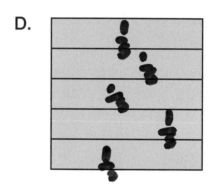

E.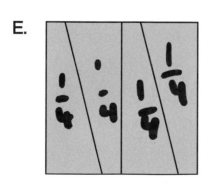

F.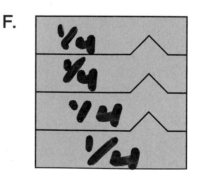

2. Fifteen students in Ms. Buckley's class study musical instruments. One-third of them study violin, one-third study French horn, and one-third study clarinet. What number of students study each instrument?

3. Billy has a bag of marbles. Half of them are blue, and half of them are red. He counts the blue marbles and he finds he has 18 of them. How many marbles does he have altogether?

4. How many minutes in $\frac{1}{2}$ hour?

5. How many minutes in $\frac{1}{3}$ hour?

6. How many minutes in $\frac{1}{4}$ hour?

7. How many minutes in one and a half hours?

8. Ovid thinks that 1/4 pizza + 1/4 pizza = 2/8 pizza. He makes this picture to show he's right.

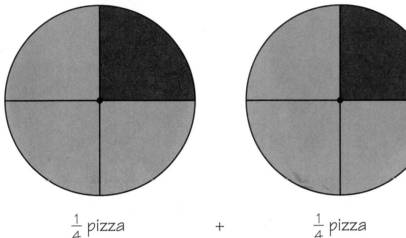

$\frac{1}{4}$ pizza   + $\frac{1}{4}$ pizza   = $\frac{2}{8}$ pizza

Michelle doesn't think Ovid is right. What do you think? Explain.

I think Ovid is right because . . .

$1 + 1 = \frac{2}{8} = ADD$
$4 + 4$

Unit 14
Collecting and Using Data

	Student Guide	Discovery Assignment Book	Adventure Book	Unit Resource Guide*
Lesson 1				
Time Again	@			@
Lesson 2				
Time and Time Again	@	@		
Lesson 3				
Tracking Our Reading	@			
Lesson 4				
Make Your Own Survey	@			
Lesson 5				
Reviewing Addition and Subtraction	@			@

Unit Resource Guide pages are from the teacher materials.

Time Again

There are many kinds of clocks. Before mechanical clocks were invented, people around the world told time in different ways. One of the earliest clocks in ancient Egypt used the shadows cast by the sun.

At first, people used a shadow clock. This clock had to be turned toward the east in the morning and toward the west in the afternoon. Later, the sundial was developed. Sundials use a round face and the shadow of a tall object to tell the time. Sundials were used in Egypt, India, Babylonia, China, Greece, and many other places.

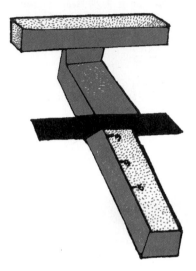

People still use sundials as decorations in gardens. When can you use a sundial?

In early China and Greece, people used water clocks to tell time. Ancient people in many other parts of the world also used water clocks. In a water clock, water flows from one pot into another pot or pots. A device inside the bottom jar—either a scale or a float—shows the time according to the amount of the water in the jar.

Chinese water clock

Greek water clock

An hourglass measures time by having sand sift through a small hole in the middle of a container.

Can you think of a reason that a water clock might be more convenient than a sundial?

Write the time shown on each clock.

1.

~~█████████~~

10:02

2.

8:26

3.

10:38

4.

7:

5.

6.

7.

8.

9.

Mary Joy's watch showed 2:35 when she left school. It showed 3:15 when she got home. How long did it take her to get home?

2:35

3:15

I found the answer by skip counting by fives. 2:40, 2:45, 2:50, 2:55, 3:00. That's 25 minutes so far. 3:05, 3:10, 3:15. That's another 15 minutes. 25 + 15 = 40 minutes. It took Mary Joy 40 minutes to get home.

I can find out how long by adding one hour then counting back. 2:35 plus sixty minutes is 3:35. That's later than she got home, so I have to count back. 3:30, 3:25, 3:20, 3:15. That's 20 minutes. So, Mary Joy got home 20 minutes less than one hour. It took Mary Joy 40 minutes to get home.

Complete the following problems.

10. Wilona looked at her watch before and after soccer practice. It showed the following times:

Before

After

How long was Wilona's practice?

---

11. Seth looked at his watch before and after gymnastics. It showed the following times:

Before

After

How long was Seth's gymnastics practice?

12. Lance went to the store for groceries. He left his apartment at 4:15. He returned home at 4:50. How long did it take Lance to get groceries?

13. Polly went to the park at 10:30 A.M. She returned home at 1:25 P.M. How long was Polly at the park?

14. Rodrigo said it took him 90 minutes to do his homework.
    A. How long is 90 minutes in hours and minutes?
    B. If Rodrigo started his homework at 4:15, what time did he finish?

15. Meghan said it took her 130 minutes to do her homework.
    A. How long is 130 minutes in hours and minutes?
    B. If Meghan started her homework at 3:30, what time did she finish?

16. Sherry's watch shows 3:10. What time was it one hour and 5 minutes ago?

17. Dana's watch shows 5:40. What time was it two hours and 20 minutes ago?

18. Danielle's watch showed 11:25. Later, it showed 12:30. How much time has passed?

19. Jeff's watch shows 7:55. Earlier, it showed 4:45. How much time has passed?

20. Do an activity for 5 minutes. If you have an analog clock, use it to tell the time you start and the time you finish. Write both times down. These are some good activities to try: reading, practicing math facts, listening to music, practicing a musical instrument, practicing a sport, running, cleaning your room, and doing chores.

Extension

You can make your own water clock by following these directions.

Materials

- a clear jar with straight sides (A peanut butter jar works well.)
- a large plastic jug with a cap (A milk bottle or soda bottle will do.)
- a hammer and a small nail
- masking tape
- a pair of scissors
- a clock
- food coloring (optional)

Instructions

1. Put a strip of tape from the top to the bottom of your jar, as shown.
2. With an adult's help, use the hammer and nail to make a small hole in the cap of the jug.

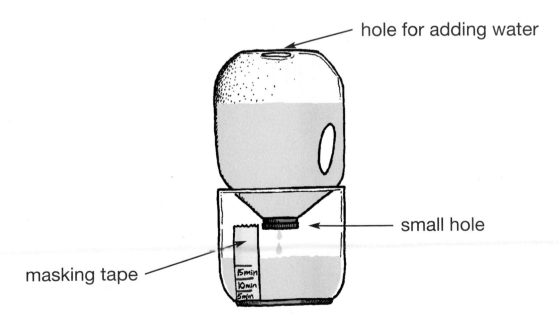

hole for adding water

small hole

masking tape

15min
10min
5min

3. Put the cap back on the jug.

4. In the bottom of the jug, make a hole large enough so that water can pour through.

5. Turn the jug upside down, and cover the hole in the cap with your finger.

6. Add water to the jug.

7. Place the jug on top of the jar as shown.

8. Let the water drip through the hole in the cap. After 5 minutes, make a mark on the masking tape showing the water level. Keep making marks every 5 minutes for a half hour.

9. Check your clock by emptying the jar and letting the water drip through again. The water should reach each mark at the same time it did before.

In ancient Rome, water clocks were used to time speeches made by lawyers in court. How could you use your clock?

Time and Time Again

This is a game for two or three players.

Materials

- 1 set of *Time and Time Again Analog Cards*
- 1 set of *Time and Time Again Digital Cards*

Rules

1. Mix the two decks together thoroughly.

2. Spread out all the cards face down on a table or desk. (If you have played the card games *Concentration* or *Lotto* before, this is similar.)

3. The first player turns over two cards at a time.

4. He or she tries to match an analog clock face with the digital time, as in this picture.

5. If the cards match, the player places them in his or her pile and takes another turn.

6. If the cards do not match, the player's turn is over. He or she should return the two cards to their original face-down position.

7. Players take turns until all the matches are found.

8. The player with the most pairs at the end of the game is the winner.

Tracking Our Reading

Mr. Wright's class kept track of their reading for one week. Each student counted the number of pages he or she read and reported the number to the class. Altogether the class read 932 pages during the week.

They set a goal of reading 2000 pages during the next two weeks. They kept track of their progress using a percentage "thermometer."

This is how the thermometer looked after they had worked toward their goal for one week. They have one more week to go.

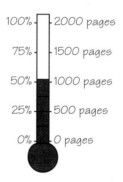

1. The class chose a goal for two weeks based on the 932 pages they read in one week. Did they choose a realistic goal? Why or why not?

2. All of their goal is the same as 100%. If they meet their goal, how many pages must they read?

3. Half of their goal is the same as 50% of their goal. How many pages must they read to reach 50% of their goal?

4. One-fourth of their goal is the same as 25%. How many pages must they read to reach 25% of their goal?

5. Three-fourths of their goal is the same as 75%. How many pages must they read to reach 75% of their goal?

6. Do you think Mr. Wright's class will reach their goal by the end of the two weeks? Why or why not?

You and your class will choose a reading goal and show your progress using percentages.

Make Your Own Survey

A **survey** is an investigation made by collecting information and then analyzing it. A third-grade class conducted surveys in their classroom to learn about each other. What type of survey do you think this student conducted?

1. Here is a picture Asha drew to show what her group wanted to learn from their survey. What did Asha's group want to learn?

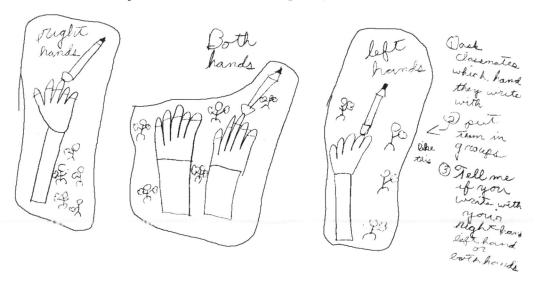

2. A. Here is the picture Rueben drew. What variable did his group study?

Number of people   toothpaste

B. What were the possible values for the variable Rueben studied in his survey?

In this lab, you will use the TIMS Laboratory Method to learn something about your classmates.

3. Choose one variable you want to study about your classmates.

Draw

4. Draw a picture or write a paragraph that explains what you are going to study and how you are going to organize your experiment.

Make Your Own Survey

Collect

5. Collect and organize your data.

Graph

6. Display your data in a graph.

Explore

7. Discuss your results in a paragraph. Your paragraph should answer the following questions:

   A. What variable did you study in your survey?

   B. What were the possible values for the variable?

   C. What did your data tell you about your classmates?

   D. Were your results as you expected or did they surprise you? Explain.

8. Use your data to make up two problems for your classmates to solve. Write the problems so that they will have to read your graph or examine your data table to find the answer.

Survey Questions

9. Julia's group chose the variable *hair color* for their survey. Here is their data table. Do you think they chose good values to write in the data table? Why or why not?

Hair Color

Hair Color	N
dark brown	卌 ||||
light brown	|||
blonde	卌
black	||
golden	卌

Robert made a survey to help the principal plan for lunch period. Then, he graphed the data and gave it to the principal. Use Robert's graph to answer Questions 10–15.

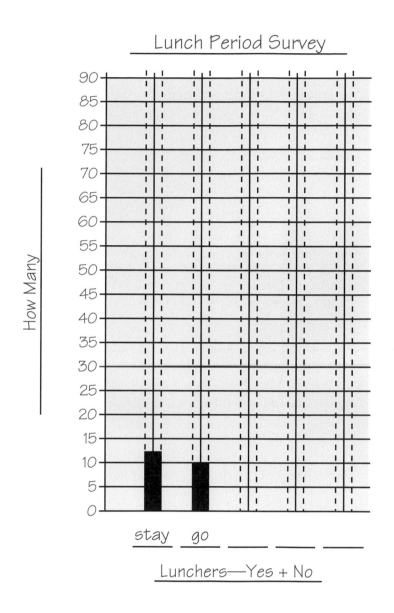

Lunch Period Survey

How Many

stay go

Lunchers—Yes + No

10. How many students stay at school for lunch?

11. How many students go home for lunch?

12. Is Robert's graph labeled correctly? Why or why not?

13. Do you think Robert used a good scale on the vertical axis? What scale would you have used?

14. What might happen if Robert did not report accurate data?

15. Robert surveyed just the students in his classroom. There are 100 students in all of the school's third-grade classrooms. Make a prediction about how many of the school's third-graders go home for lunch and how many stay at school.

Reviewing Addition and Subtraction

Ms. Carney's class collected data on their reading for a week. The class read 665 minutes on Monday and 475 minutes on Tuesday. To find the total number of minutes the class read on both days, Ethan used base-ten pieces to help him add 665 and 475.

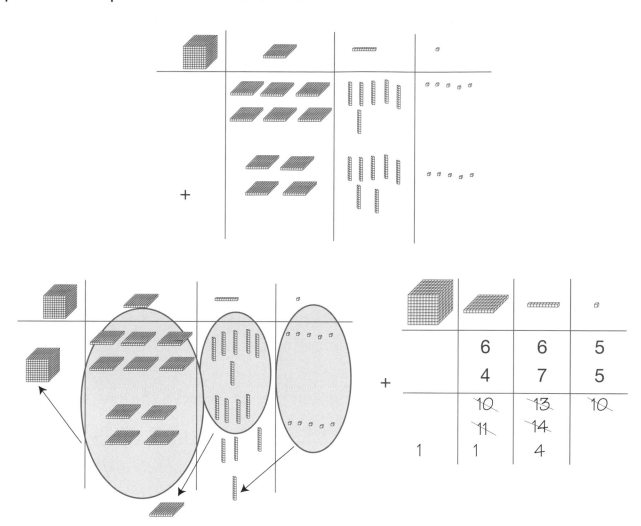

1. Ethan said the answer is 114. Was he correct? If not, what is the correct answer? Explain.

2. Show how to solve the problem using pencil and paper.

Sam wanted to know how many pages the class read over the weekend. The class read 89 pages on Saturday and 147 pages on Sunday.

He used base-ten pieces to help him find the answer. Then, he used base-ten shorthand to explain to the class what he did.

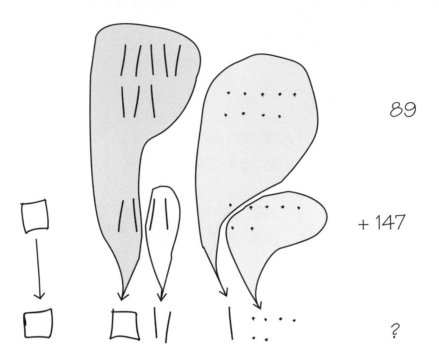

89

+ 147

?

3. What is Sam's answer to the problem? Do you think he is correct? Why or why not?

4. Explain how Sam used the base-ten pieces to solve the problem.

Sam also used pencil and paper to solve the problem. Here is what he wrote down:

$$\begin{array}{r} 89 \\ +\ 147 \\ \underline{\scriptstyle 1\ 1} \\ 236 \end{array}$$

5. What do the little ones stand for?

6. How would you solve the problem?

Reviewing Addition and Subtraction

Ms. Carney's class read 2038 pages in a week. Mrs. Lee's class read 1652 pages during the same week. Ms. Carney's class wanted to know how many more pages they read than Mrs. Lee's class did. Nelle used the base-ten pieces to find the answer with subtraction.

First, she set up the number 2038 with base-ten pieces.

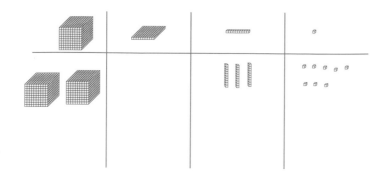

Then, Nelle thought about how to subtract 1652 from 2038.

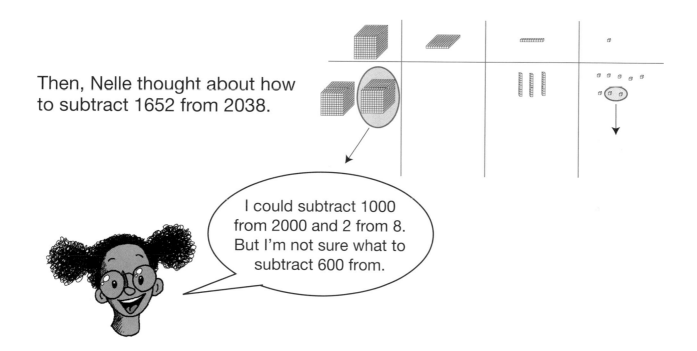

I could subtract 1000 from 2000 and 2 from 8. But I'm not sure what to subtract 600 from.

7. What should Nelle do to solve the problem?

Nelle decided to trade base-ten pieces.

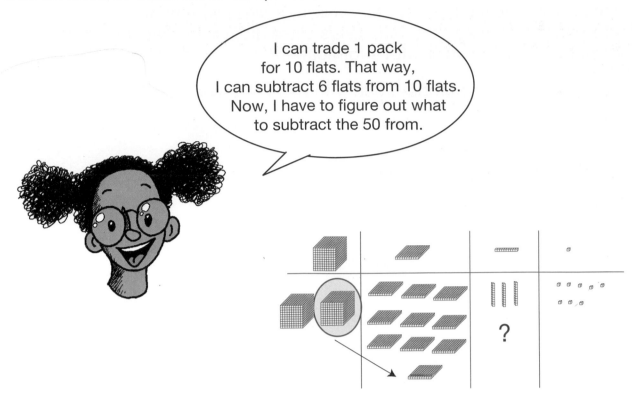

I can trade 1 pack
for 10 flats. That way,
I can subtract 6 flats from 10 flats.
Now, I have to figure out what
to subtract the 50 from.

8. What pieces did Nelle trade next?

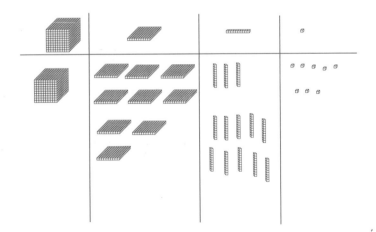

9. Look at Nelle's pieces. Do they still represent the original number, 2038? How do you know?

10. What is the answer to Nelle's problem?

11. Check the answer by solving the problem another way.

Reviewing Addition and Subtraction

Pages and Minutes

Solve Questions 12–15 in two ways. Use paper and pencil and base-ten pieces or base-ten shorthand. Estimate to be sure your answers are reasonable.

12. 4765
    + 3829

13. 803
    − 527

14. 6409
    − 2576

15. 648
    + 896

16. Explain a mental math method for Question 13.

17. Explain your estimation strategy for Question 14.

For Questions 18–24, follow these steps:

- Try to say the problem in your own words.
- Solve the problem. You may use paper and pencil, base-ten pieces, or mental math.
- Be sure to write a number sentence for the problem.
- Look back. Does your answer make sense?

---

18. Ms. Carney's class read 226 pages on Thursday and 284 pages on Friday.

   A. How many pages did the class read on both days?

   B. How many more pages did the class read on Friday than on Thursday?

19. Ms. Carney's class read for 905 minutes on Saturday and for 715 minutes on Sunday. How many more minutes did the class read on Saturday?

20. On Wednesday, Ms. Carney's class read for 600 minutes. How many hours is this?

21. A. The class read 210 pages on Monday, 151 pages on Tuesday, and 190 pages on Wednesday. What was the total number of pages the class read from Monday through Wednesday?

   B. On Thursday the class read 245 pages and on Friday the class read 177 pages. What was the total number of pages the class read on Thursday and Friday together?

   C. How many pages did the class read in the entire week?

---

22. Mr. Rodriguez's class is trying to read 1500 pages in one week. They have read 1301 pages so far. How many more pages will they have to read to meet their goal?

23. Mrs. Lee's class is trying to read 1500 pages also. They have read 1158 pages so far. How many more pages do they need to read to meet the goal?

24. A. How many more pages had Mr. Rodriguez's class read than Mrs. Lee's class?

    B. How many pages have Mr. Rodriguez's class and Mrs. Lee's class read altogether?

For Questions 25 and 26, you will need to use data from your class data table. Copy each problem on your paper. Fill in the blanks with data from your class data table. Then, solve the problems.

25. We read _____ pages on _____ and _____ ges on

_____ . How many pages did we read on both days?

26. We read for _____ minutes on _____ and for

minutes on _____ . How many more minutes did

_____ than _____ ?

Homework

1. Add 478 to each number below. Before you add, estimate answer.

    A. 25   **B.** 319   **C.** 2035

2. Subtract 478 from each number below. Before you subtract, estimate each answer.

    A. 869   **B.** 1227   **C.** 1500

For Questions 3–6, solve the problem. Estimate to be sure your answer is reasonable.

3. At Lucero School, there are 129 students in third grade, 138 students in fourth grade, and 144 students in fifth grade. How many students are in the three grades?

4. At King School, there are 1047 students. There are 877 students at Lucero School.

   A. How many students go to these two schools?

   B. How many more students go to King School than Lucero School?

   C. Explain your estimation strategy for Question 4A.

   D. Explain a method for Question 4B using mental math.

5. Lucero School bought 1000 folders so that each student could be given one on the first day of school. How many folders will they have left over?

6. The principal at Lucero School figured out that the school needs 7029 textbooks for all the grades. Right now, the school has 5634 textbooks. How many more textbooks does the principal need to order?

For Questions 7–10, solve each problem in two ways. You may use mental math, paper and pencil, or base-ten shorthand. Estimate to be sure your answers are reasonable.

7.   1530
    + 3492

8.   296
   − 178

9.   6376
   − 4584

10.   7102
    + 4367

Unit 15
DECIMAL INVESTIGATIONS

	Student Guide	Discovery Assignment Book	Adventure Book	Unit Resource Guide*
Lesson 1				
Decimal Fractions	@	@		
Lesson 2				
Measuring to the Nearest Tenth	@	@		@
Lesson 3				
Decimal Hex		@		
Lesson 4				
Length vs. Number	@			
Lesson 5				
Nothing to It!	@			

Unit Resource Guide pages are from the teacher materials.

Decimal Fractions

You will need your base-ten pieces for this activity. You will use base-ten shorthand to show your work with the base-ten pieces. The table below shows the base-ten shorthand. Before, a bit was one whole. **Now, a flat will be one whole.**

Base-Ten Pieces	Name	Base-Ten Shorthand	Description	Common Fraction	Decimal Fraction
(flat grid)	flat	(square)	one whole	1	1.0
(skinny)	skinny	/	one tenth	$\frac{1}{10}$	0.1
□	bit	·	one one-hundredth	$\frac{1}{100}$	0.01

1. What fraction of a flat is one skinny?

2. What fraction of a flat is one bit?

When the flat is one whole, then two skinnies are two-tenths. The common fraction for two-tenths is $\frac{2}{10}$, and the decimal fraction is 0.2.

3. **A.** If the flat is one whole, then what are three skinnies? Write a decimal and a common fraction for three skinnies.

   B. Write a decimal and a common fraction for seven skinnies.

   C. Write a decimal and a common fraction for nine skinnies.

4. Count by tenths again using skinnies: one tenth, two tenths, three tenths...

    A. What happens when you get more than ten skinnies?

    B. Fill in the chart on your *Tenths Helper* Activity Page by writing common and decimal fractions for tenths.

    C. What happens to decimal fractions after you write 0.9?

5. Use a calculator to count by 0.1s: 0.1, 0.2, 0.3.... What happens after 0.9?

The flat can be divided into smaller pieces. It can be divided into bits.

6. How many bits are in a flat?

A bit is one one-hundredth of a flat. We write this as $\frac{1}{100}$ or 0.01.

$$\boxed{} = 1 \qquad \square = \frac{1}{100} \text{ or } 0.01$$

Money

Bits, skinnies, and flats can be used to show different amounts of money. A dollar is the whole, so a flat can be used for a dollar. A bit can be used for a penny since there are 100 pennies in a dollar.

7. **A.** How many dimes are in one dollar?

    B. What fraction of one dollar is one dime?

    C. What base-ten piece can stand for a dime?

Two dollars and thirty-six cents can be shown with base-ten pieces.

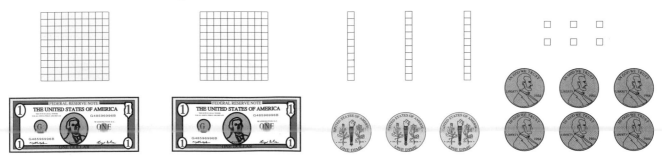

Two dollars and thirty-six cents is written as $2.36 as a decimal fraction.

Ninety-eight cents can be shown with base-ten pieces and written as $0.98.

8. Use your base-ten pieces to help you write the following amounts as decimal fractions. Show your work with base-ten pieces with base-ten shorthand.

A. seventy-three cents

B. three dollars and twelve cents

C. thirteen cents

D. one dollar and seven cents

Tenths, Tenths, Tenths

This is a game for two people. For this game, a flat is one whole.

Materials

- base-ten pieces (flats and skinnies)
- a table with headings like the table below

Base-Ten Shorthand	Fraction of a Flat	
	Common	**Decimal**
▢ |/|	$1\frac{3}{10}$	1.3
|/| |/ |/|/| |/ ||/	$\frac{16}{10}$	1.6
▢ ▢ /||/	$2\frac{5}{10}$	2.5

Rules

- The first player makes a number with skinnies and flats and shows it in the table using base-ten shorthand.
- The second player has to write the common and decimal fractions for the number and then say the number. If the second player is right, he or she gets one point.
- Players continue to take turns making numbers and writing and saying numbers.

In this game, you are allowed to be tricky: You don't have to use the Fewest Pieces Rule when you are working with the base-ten pieces, but you must use the rule when writing decimal fractions. How do you write this number as a decimal fraction?

Sample Play

Rita and John were playing *Tenths, Tenths, Tenths*. Rita tried to trick John by making this number:

For his fractions, John wrote $\frac{12}{10}$ and 0.12. He said, "Twelve-tenths."

Rita thought that John was wrong, but she couldn't explain why.

What do you think?

Measuring to the Nearest Tenth

Marta likes to make jewelry with small beads. She has made a necklace and a bracelet that match.

Now, Marta has decided to make a matching ring to complete her jewelry set. To do this, she needs to know how long to make the ring. She decides to use a piece of string to measure her finger and then to measure that piece of string with a ruler.

Marta looks at the string and the ruler and decides that her finger is about five centimeters around. She makes her ring 5 cm around, but when she tries it on she is disappointed. She discovers that her ring is too big. She can't wear it because it falls off.

As Marta discovered, measuring to the **nearest** centimeter (the closest centimeter) is not always exact enough. Even measuring to the nearest half centimeter may not be exact enough. Marta's method would have worked if she had measured to the nearest tenth of a centimeter. Now, you are going to learn to measure to the nearest tenth of a centimeter.

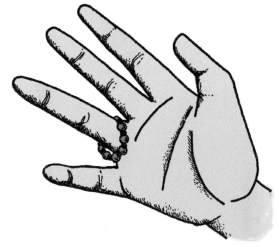

Reading a Centimeter Ruler

If you look carefully at a centimeter ruler, you can see small lines between each centimeter. Here is what part of a centimeter ruler might look like through a magnifying glass.

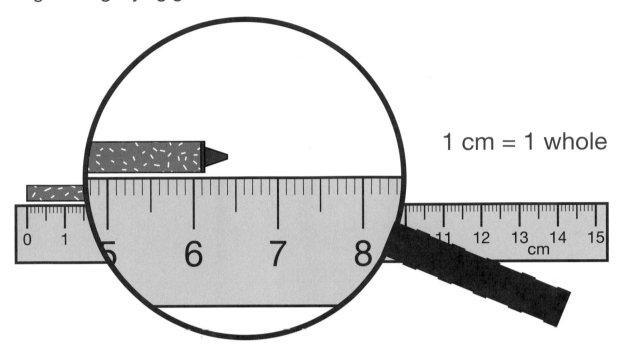

1 cm = 1 whole

Each small space between the whole centimeters is one-tenth of a centimeter. The end of the crayon is between 6 and 7 cm. You can count how many tenths past 6 cm the end of the crayon is. We call this $6\frac{4}{10}$ cm or 6.4 cm.

Look at Marta's string. Using tenths of a centimeter, can you tell her how long around she should make her ring so that it fits?

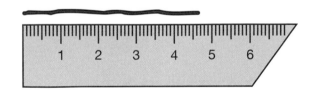

Measure the length of each row of hexagons to the nearest centimeter and then to the nearest half-centimeter.

1.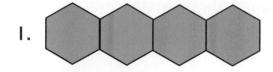

2.

3.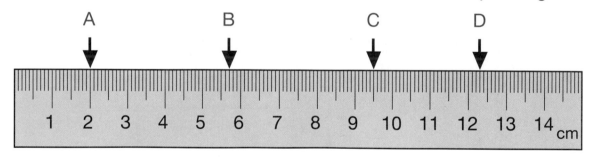

4. What centimeter measurements are the arrows pointing to?

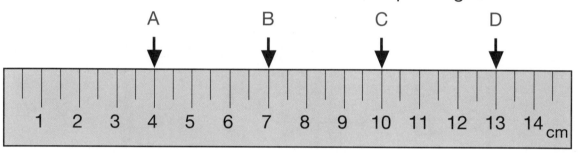

5. What centimeter or tenth of a centimeter are the arrows pointing to?

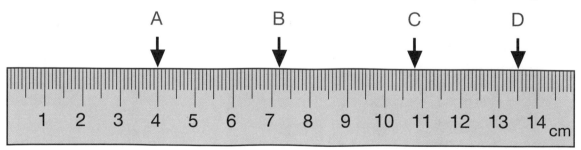

6. What centimeter or tenth of a centimeter are the arrows pointing to?

7. Here is a picture of a rectangle and a ruler.
   A. Measure the length of the rectangle to the nearest centimeter.
   B. Measure the length of the rectangle to the nearest tenth of a centimeter.

8. Maria did not line up the end of her ruler with the end of the rectangle.
   A. How could she still measure its length?
   B. What is its length?

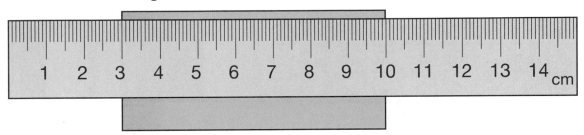

9. Here is another rectangle that is not lined up with the end of the ruler. What is its width to the nearest tenth of a centimeter?

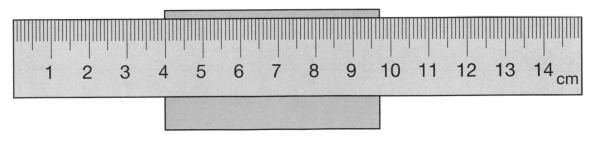

Sometimes, rulers get broken or worn at the ends. You can still use such rulers to measure length.

10. What is the width of each rectangle to the nearest tenth of a centimeter?
    A.

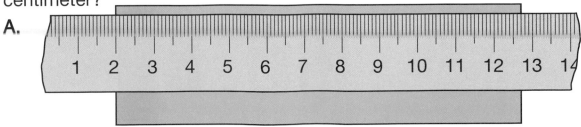

B.

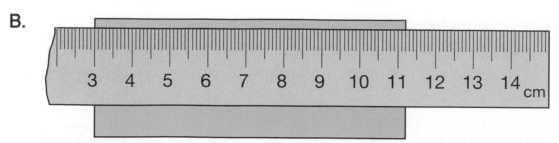

C.

11. Measure the length, width, and diagonal of this rectangle to the nearest tenth of a centimeter.

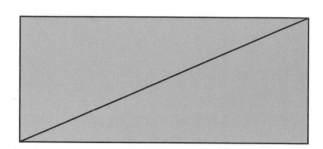

Measure these pencils to the nearest tenth of a centimeter.

12.

13.

14.

15. Find the length, width, and diagonal of this book to the nearest tenth of a centimeter.

Length vs. Number

Roberto collects pop cans. On his vacation, he visited Chicago. He thought the Sears Tower was really cool. After going up to the Skydeck, he thought about how many soda pop cans it would take to make a stack as tall as the Sears Tower.

The next day, Roberto went to the Planetarium. Before seeing a show about stars and planets, Roberto bought a pack of gum at a vending machine. As he watched the show, he began to wonder how many sticks of gum would reach around the world.

Jackie collects baseball cards. On her vacation, her family went to Baltimore. Her dad took her to an Orioles game. After seeing the game, Jackie began to wonder how many baseball cards would fit edge to edge between home plate and first base.

While in Baltimore, Jackie's mom found out that Adam Ant was having a concert nearby. (Her mom liked to listen to this band when she was younger.) The family decided to go to the concert together. Jackie's brother, Jamal, has an ant farm. As they stood in line to buy the tickets, Jackie wondered how long a line of 1000 ants would be.

How would you solve the problems Roberto and Jackie thought up on their vacations? In this lab, you will learn ways to answer questions like these. You will use the TIMS Laboratory Method to study two variables: the Number of Objects in a row *(N)* and the Length of the row *(L)*.

You will measure the length of rows with different numbers of objects. You might measure three rows of 4, 8, and 12 pennies; or you might measure five rows of 1, 2, 4, 8, and 16 paper clips. There are many objects that you can use. A few that work well are plastic connecting links, brass washers, baseball cards, paper clips, and sticks of gum. After you decide what objects to use, you will decide how many rows you will make and how many of your objects to put in your rows. Your teacher will help you choose.

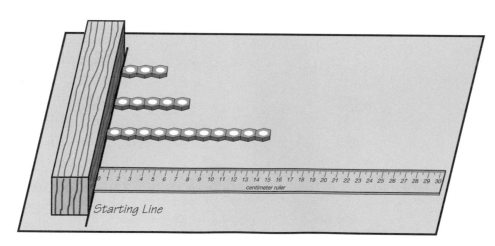

Draw a labeled picture of the experiment setup.

1. What are the two main variables in this lab?

2. Which variable has values that you can choose?

3. Which variable has values that you don't know at the beginning of the lab?

4. Roberto used baseball cards for his experiment. This is how he lined them up. What do you think about Roberto's work?

Work with your group to measure rows of your objects. Make rows with different Numbers of Objects (N) and measure the Length of each row (L) to the nearest 0.1 cm. Before you begin, you will need to consider these questions:

- How many different rows will you make?
- What Number of Objects (N) will you have in each row (what values of N will you use)?
- How many times will you measure each row (how many trials will you make)?

Design your own data table for recording your data.

5. How long is a row of objects with zero objects in the row? (When the Number of Objects, $N = 0$, what is the Length L?) Add this point to your graph.

Graph your data. Use a ruler. Before you start, your group will need to decide how to number the axes. Numbering the axis labeled "Length" is tricky because your measurements have decimals. Discuss with your group what you should do.

6. Is a straight line a good fit for your data? If so, use a ruler to draw a best-fit line. Be sure to include the point you added in Question 5.

7. Use your graph to predict the length of a row of three objects. Then, check your prediction. How close was your prediction?

8. Use your graph to predict the length of a row of five objects. Check your prediction. How close was your prediction?

9. **A.** What is the length of a row of 50 of your objects? Explain how you found your answer.

   B. What is the length of a row of 100 of your objects? Explain how you found your answer.

10. Sandra and José each did the experiment. José used big paper clips. Sandra used small ones. Which line on the graph (A or B) is the line for the big paper clips? Explain.

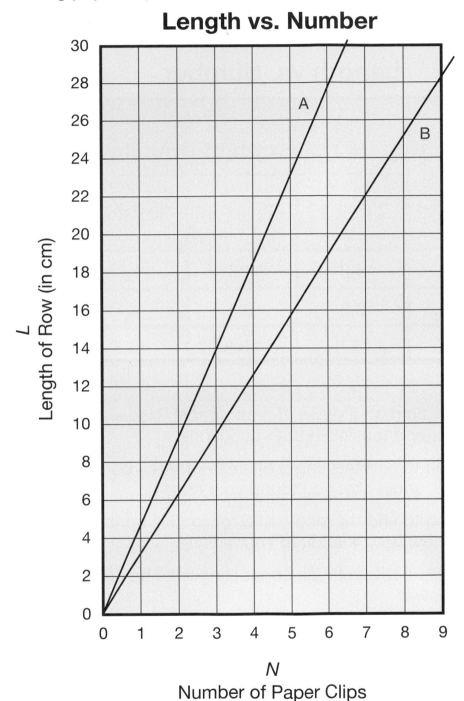

Length vs. Number

L
Length of Row (in cm)

N
Number of Paper Clips

Homework

Jaime did *Length vs. Number* using connecting links. He placed the links flat, laying them end to end. Here is his data.

Length vs. Number

N Number of Links in Row	L Length of Row (in cm)			
	Trial 1	Trial 2	Trial 3	Median
1	4.2	4.3	4.2	4.2
2	8.5	8.4	8.4	8.4
4	16.9	16.8	16.9	16.9

1. Graph Jaime's data on a piece of graph paper. Use a ruler to fit a line to the data. Extend the line in both directions.

2. Use your graph to find the length of a row of three connecting links. On your graph, show how you found your answer.

3. Use your graph to find the length of a row of five connecting links. On your graph, show how you found your answer.

4. How long would a row with ten connecting links be? Explain how you found your answer.

Nothing to It!

This is a game for two or more players.

Materials

- 2 number decks (with digits 1 through 10) or playing cards

Rules

The goal is to get the most cards.

1. The dealer gives each player four cards.

2. With playing cards, the face cards all count as 10.

3. Each player adds or subtracts the four cards in his or her hand to get the smallest possible result. The players write down their number sentences.

4. Players may not have number sentences with numbers less than zero.

5. The player with the smallest total takes all the cards from that round.

6. The dealer gives each player four more cards. The players continue making number sentences and giving all their cards to the player with the smallest answer.

7. Players continue until all the cards are gone. The player with the most cards is the winner.

Sample Round

Ella and Richard are playing *Nothing to It!* Suppose that Ella has the cards 4, 9, 2, and 7 and that Richard has the cards 4, 6, 8, and 4.

Ella could make $4 + 7 - 9 - 2 = 0$.

The best Richard could do is $4 + 8 - 6 - 4 = 2$.

Ella's hand   Richard's hand

Since 0 is smaller than 2, Ella would take all eight cards.

Unit 16

VOLUME

	Student Guide	Discovery Assignment Book	Adventure Book	Unit Resource Guide*
Lesson 1				
Measuring Volume	◎			
Lesson 2				
Fill 'er Up!	◎			
Lesson 3				
Volume Hunt		◎		
Lesson 4				
Elixir of Youth			◎	
Lesson 5				
Paying Taxes Problems	◎			

Unit Resource Guide pages are from the teacher materials.

Measuring Volume

Which is heavier, one pound of popcorn or a one-pound rock?

I've heard that riddle before. They both have the same weight—one pound!

Yeah. The difference between them is their volume.

What is volume?

Volume is a measurement of size. It is the amount of space that an object takes up. If the object is a container, like a box or a bottle, then the volume is the amount of space inside it.

A common metric unit of volume is the cubic centimeter. A **cubic centimeter (cc)** is the volume of a cube that is 1 centimeter long on each side.

A **milliliter** is another metric unit of volume. It is the same as 1 cubic centimeter.

A **liter (l)** is a metric unit used to measure the volume of large objects. One liter holds 1000 milliliters. It also holds 1000 cubic centimeters.

Jason thinks that 2000 cubic centimeters is the same as 1000 milliliters. Shanila thinks it's the same as 2000 milliliters. Do you know who is right?

The volume is 2 liters.

That's the same as 2000 milliliters.

How many cubic centimeters is that?

1. Build these shapes with your cubes. Find the volume by counting the number of cubes. The volume will be in cubic centimeters.

A.

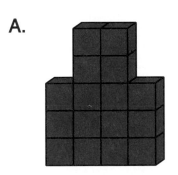

B.

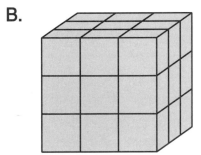

C.

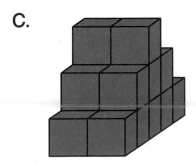

D.

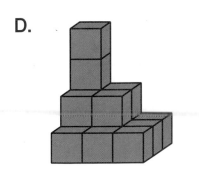

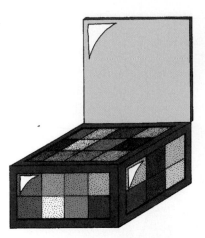

Jason used his centimeter cubes to find the volume of this box. He found the volume was 24 cubic centimeters. Explain how he found the volume.

Estimating Volume

Shanila estimated the volume of a marker by building a model of it from her centimeter connecting cubes. She estimated that the volume was about 14 cubic centimeters.

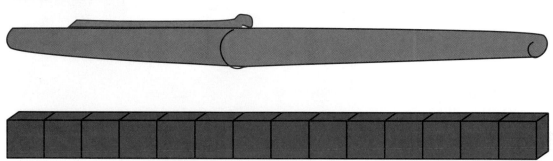

2. Use centimeter connecting cubes to estimate volumes as Shanila did. Make models of at least four objects. Your teacher will help you choose objects. One of your objects should be a shape you make from 10 centimeter connecting cubes as shown in the table below. Record your estimates in a data table like the one below. Shanila's data for the marker is shown. (Keep your data table. You will need it for later.)

O Object	*E* Estimated Volume from Cube Model	
Marker	14 cc	

Measuring the Volume of Liquids

When we measure liquids like water and milk, we often use a measuring cup. Scientists use graduated cylinders to measure volume.

To read the level of water in a graduated cylinder, bend down and **put your eyes at the level of the top of the water.** In this picture, only Shanila is reading the water level correctly. **Tell why.**

It looks like 82 cc from where I stand.

It looks like 80 cc to me!

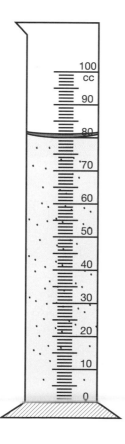

Water creeps up the sides of a graduated cylinder. It makes a curved surface at the top called a **meniscus.** The meniscus makes it look as though there are two lines on top of each other. You should always *read the lower line.* The lower line shows the level of the water. This cylinder shows a meniscus with a water level of 80 cc. (The meniscus will be more noticeable with glass graduated cylinders than with plastic graduated cylinders.)

Measuring Volume

Measuring the Volume of Solid Objects

How can we find the volume of a solid object, such as a rock? A scientist might put the object under water in a graduated cylinder and see how much the water rises.

To find the volume of a rock, Shanila and Jason first put 50 cubic centimeters of water in a graduated cylinder.

Let's start with 50 cc of water. I'll use an eyedropper to put in the last few drops.

Then, they slid the rock into the cylinder.

The rock made the water rise from 50 to 63 cubic centimeters.

That means the volume of the rock is 13 cubic centimeters.

How did Jason find the volume of the rock?

3. Measure the actual volume of each of the objects you used in Question 2 by holding each object under water in a graduated cylinder. How much higher does the water rise? Record each volume in the last column of your data table.

O Object	E Estimated Volume from Cube Model	V Volume by Displacement
	14 cc	12 cc

Homework

Look at the two scales on this page. Write the number for each letter.

I.

100

90

A → 80

70

B → 60

C →

50

D → 40

E →

30

F → 20

10

0

2.

A → 120

B → 100

80

C →

60

D →

40

E → 20

F →

0

3. Tasha put a piece of clay under water in a graduated cylinder. What was the volume of the clay?

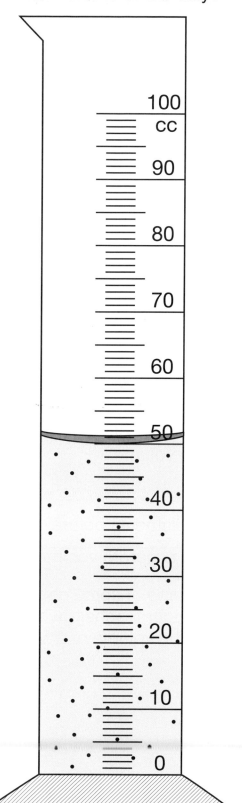 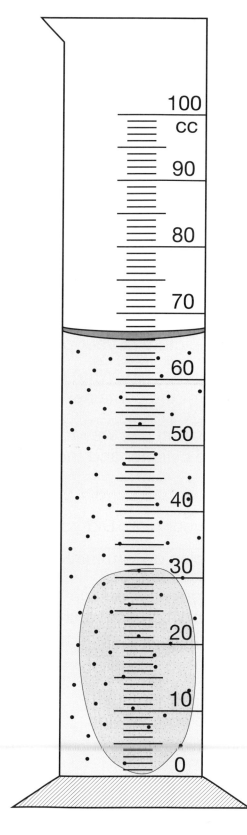

Fill 'er Up!

Andrea found two jars with unusual shapes.

Work with a partner or your group. Help Andrea make a plan to find out which jar has a greater volume.

Get a container, a graduated cylinder, and some water from your teacher. Pretend that the container is one of Andrea's jars. How can you use the graduated cylinder and the water to find the volume of the container?

I think this jar is bigger, but how can I be sure?

1. Draw a picture of your plan.

2. Follow your plan. What is the volume of the container?

There is more than one way to find the volume. Think of another way to use the graduated cylinder and the water to find the volume.

3. Draw a picture of your second plan.

4. Follow your plan. Did you get the same volume as before?

5. Which plan do you think gave you a more accurate volume? Why?

We will carry out an investigation to find the volume of some containers. You will find the volume of at least three containers your teacher gives you. Later, you can use this information to guess and find the volume of a Mystery Jar.

The Lab

Draw a picture that shows how you will find the volume of your containers. In your picture, write the sizes and shapes of your containers and the names you will give them in the data table.

Find the volume of at least three containers of different sizes. Your measurements may contain some experimental error. So, you should measure the volume of each container at least three times and find the median. Record your data in a table like the one below.

Container	Volume in _____ unit			
	Trial 1	Trial 2	Trial 3	Median

Graph

Graph your data on a sheet of graph paper. Will you make a bar graph or a point graph?

Discuss with your group how you will label the axes so that your data will fit.

Explore

Use your data to help you answer these questions.

6. Which container has the smallest volume?

7. Which container has the largest volume?

8. **A.** Use your graph or your data to predict the number of *full* small containers you can pour into your large container. How many more cubic centimeters of water do you think you will need to fill the large container? Try to make your prediction as accurate as possible. Explain how you made your prediction.

   B. Use your equipment to check your prediction. How many *full* small containers did you pour into your largest container without it overflowing? How many more cubic centimeters of water did you need to fill the large container completely?

   C. Was your prediction close to the actual result? Why or why not?

9. Tom poured 4 full small jars of 125 cc into his large jar. Then, he filled the large jar with another 78 cc of water.

   A. What is the volume of Tom's large jar?

   B. Write an addition sentence for the volume of the large jar.

   C. Write your number sentence in a different way. This time, use multiplication and addition.

10. Molly fills her 80 cc graduated cylinder with water and empties it into a jar four times, but the jar is still not full. She fills the graduated cylinder again and uses this water to fill the jar to the top. Her graduated cylinder still has 25 cc of water in it. What is the volume of the jar? Show your work.

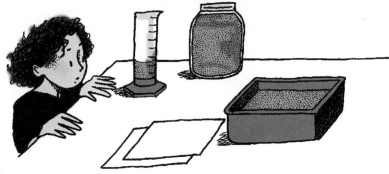

11. Mimi has a small jar with a volume of 40 cc and a bigger jar with a volume of 230 cc.

   A. How many *full* small jars of water can Mimi pour into her big jar? How much more water does she need to fill the big jar to the top? Show your work.

   B. Write a number sentence for your answer.

12. A container has a volume of 240 cc. You have many small jars, each with a volume of 45 cc. You want to pour all the water from the big container into the small jars.

   A. About how many jars can you fill? First, write down your estimate. Then, solve the problem.

   B. How much water will be in the last jar?

   C. Write a division sentence for the problem.

13. Jeff has these three jars.

  A. Do jar B and jar C have the same shape?

  B. Which is taller, jar B or jar C?

  C. Which is wider, jar B or jar C?

  D. It takes 6 jar As to fill jar B. It takes 8 jar As to fill jar C. Which has a greater volume, jar B or jar C? Why do you think so?

jar A   Smallest

jar B   middle

jar C   biggest

Paying Taxes Problems

Daniel and Maria work in the school store. They charge 6¢ tax on every dollar a student spends at the store. This is how the tax works:

If the amount is 50¢, the tax is $0.03. The cost is 53¢.
If the amount is $1.00, the tax is $0.06. The cost is $1.06.
If the amount is $1.50, the tax is $0.09. The cost is $1.59.

They use a graph to find the tax on different amounts.

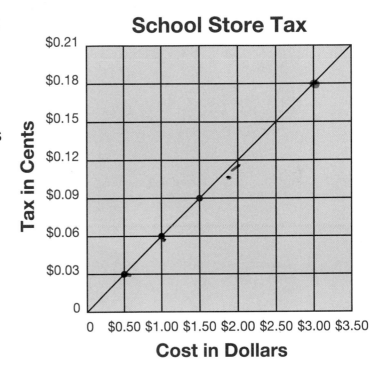

School Store Tax

Use a variety of strategies to solve these problems.

1. The price of a notebook is $3.00. What was the tax?

2. Carmen bought paper. The price was $4.50. How much tax did she pay?

3. Otis bought pencils. The price before tax was $2.50. How much did he pay altogether for the pencils and the tax?

4. Jim paid 12¢ in tax when he bought markers. What was the price of the markers before tax? With tax?

5. Brandy paid a total of $3.71 for pens and the tax. What was the price of the pens?

6. Jonah bought paper for $2.25 and erasers for $1.75. What was his total including tax?

WHOLES AND PARTS

	Student Guide	Discovery Assignment Book	Adventure Book	Unit Resource Guide*
Lesson 1				
Geoboard Fractions				
Lesson 2				
Folding Fractions				
Lesson 3				
The Clever Tailor				
Lesson 4				
Fraction Hex				

Unit Resource Guide pages are from the teacher materials.

Geoboard Fractions

Making Halves

Make this rectangle on your geoboard.

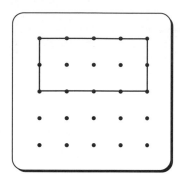

Below is one way to divide this rectangle in half. Find at least five other ways to divide the rectangle in half. Draw the ways you find on *Geoboard Paper.*

Circle ways of dividing the rectangle into halves that are the same shape.

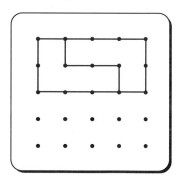

Write answers for these questions.

1. What is the area of the whole rectangle?

2. What is the area of each half?

3. Are any of your ways of dividing the rectangle "flipped" from another way?

Making Thirds

Make this rectangle on your geoboard.

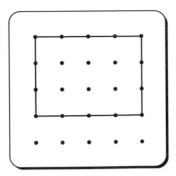

4. Below is one way to divide this rectangle in thirds. Find other ways to divide the rectangle in thirds. Draw each way you find on *Geoboard Paper.*

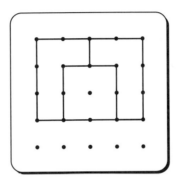

5. For each way you divided the rectangle, color all the thirds that are **congruent** (the same size and shape). Write the fraction for the amount shaded. For example, this is what you would show for the thirds above:

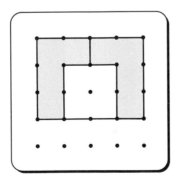 $\dfrac{2}{3}$

Making Fourths

Make this rectangle on your geoboard.

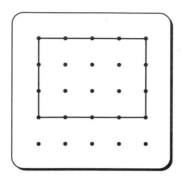

6. Fran said the picture below shows one way to divide this rectangle in quarters (fourths). Do you agree? Why or why not? Find other ways to divide the rectangle in fourths. Draw each way you find on *Geoboard Paper*.

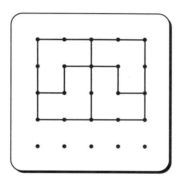

7. For each way you find, color zero, one, two, three, or four fourths. Then, write a fraction that tells how much you chose to color. For example, for Fran's fourths, you might do this:

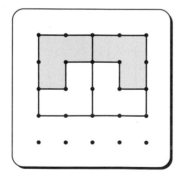

$$\frac{2}{4}$$

Folding Fractions

Folding One-third

We have many ways to name the same number. For example, we can name the number 5 by writing 1 + 4 or 2 + 3. We can also name 700 + 80 + 3 by writing the number 783. A lot of the work of arithmetic is finding other names for numbers.

We have different names for fractions, too. Another name for one-third is two-sixths. When two fractions name the same number, we say they are **equivalent**. The word *equivalent* means equal or equal value. So we can say that one-third is equivalent to two-sixths.

In this activity, you will find and name fractions that are equivalent to one-third. Follow these steps.

1. Use the *One-third Folding Sheet*. Fold it on the lines into three equal parts.

2. Unfold the paper. Then, color one of the thirds.

3. Use the One-third data table in your *Discovery Assignment Book*. It is like the one below. Fill in the first row as shown below.

One-third

Colored Parts	Total Parts	Fraction Colored
1	3	$\frac{1}{3}$

4. Now, fold the paper in half the other way as shown in the picture below. Unfold the paper and trace the folds.

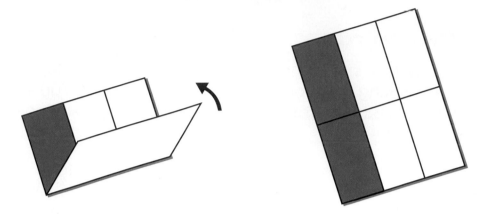

5. Count the colored parts and count all the parts. Write these numbers in the first two columns of the One-third data table. Then, in the last column write a fraction that is equivalent to one-third.

6. Fold the paper as you did in Question 4. Then, fold it in half the long way. Look at the picture below.

7. How many total parts do you think the paper will have when you unfold it?

8. Unfold the paper and trace the folds. Then, count the colored parts and the total parts. Use your paper to find another fraction that is equivalent to one-third. Fill in the third row in the One-third data table.

Now, you need to get another One-third Folding Sheet.

9. Fold the new sheet of paper in thirds the long way as you did in Question 1. Then, unfold it and color one of the thirds.

10. Fold the paper into thirds the other way. Then, unfold the paper and trace the folds.

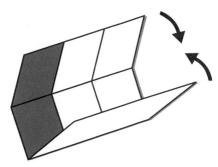

11. Count the parts and fill in another row in the One-third data table.

12. Fold the paper as you did in Question 10. Then, fold it in half the long way. Look at the picture below.

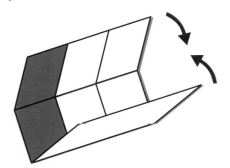 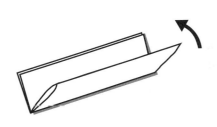

13. How many total parts do you think the paper will have when you unfold it?

14. Unfold the paper and trace the folds. Then, count the parts and fill in another row in the One-third data table.

15. The table should now have five rows filled in. What patterns do you notice?

16. A. Is $\frac{5}{15}$ equivalent to $\frac{1}{3}$? Why or why not?
    B. Find other fractions that are equivalent to one-third.

17. How do you know if a fraction is equivalent to one-third?

Folding One-half

This activity is like *Folding One-third* except that you will find fractions that are equivalent to one-half. You will need several sheets of paper.

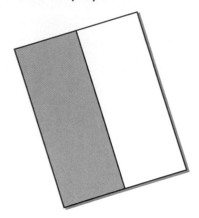

18. Get a sheet of paper. Fold the paper in half the long way. Be sure the two parts are the same size.

19. Unfold the paper, and draw a line between the halves. Then, color one of the halves.

20. Use the One-half data table in your *Discovery Assignment Book* similar to the one below. Fill in the first row as shown below.

One-half

Colored Parts	Total Parts	Fraction Colored
1	2	$\frac{1}{2}$

21. Now, fold the paper in half the other way.

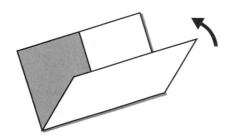

22. Unfold the paper and trace the fold. Count the colored parts and count all the parts. Write the numbers in the first two columns of the One-half data table. Then, in the last column write a fraction that is equivalent to one-half.

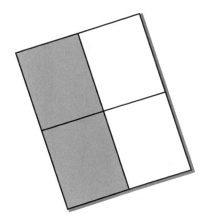

23. Fold the paper as you did in Question 21. Then, fold it in half the long way. Look at the picture below.

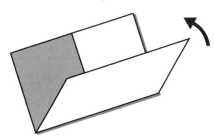 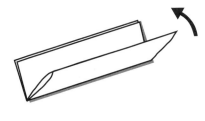

24. How many total parts do you think there will be when you unfold the paper?

25. Unfold the paper and trace the folds. Then, count the colored parts and the total parts. Use your paper to find another fraction that is equivalent to one-half. Fill in the third row in the One-half data table.

Now, you need to get another piece of paper.

26. Fold your new piece of paper in half the long way. Unfold it. Draw a line between the halves. Then, color one of the halves.

27. Fold the paper into three equal parts the other way. Then, unfold the paper and trace the folds.

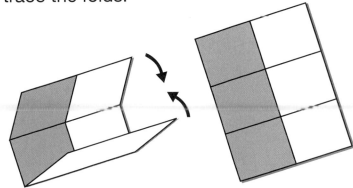

28. Count the parts and fill in another row in the One-half data table.

29. Fold the paper into thirds as you did in Question 27. Then, fold it in half the long way. Look at the picture below.

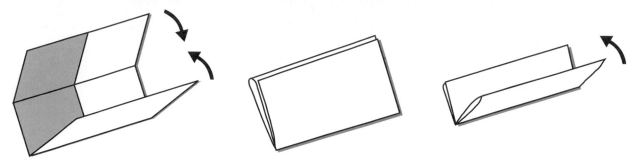

30. How many total parts do you think the paper will have when you unfold it?

31. Unfold the paper and trace the folds. Then, count the parts, and fill in another row in the One-half data table.

32. The table should now have five rows filled in. What patterns do you notice?

33. Find other fractions that are equivalent to one-half.

34. How do you know if a fraction is equivalent to one-half?

Folding One-fourth

You have folded and colored paper to find fractions that are equivalent to one-half and one-third. Now, you will fold and color paper to find fractions that are equivalent to one-fourth. You will need at least two pieces of paper.

35. Fold a sheet of paper the long way into four equal parts. To do this, fold the paper in half the long way. Then, fold it in half the long way again.

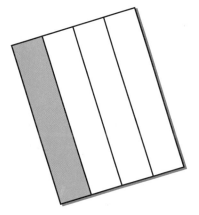

36. Use the One-fourth data table in your *Discovery Assignment Book.*
Fill in the first row as shown below. This fraction should describe the
sheet of paper that you folded and colored in Question 35.

One-fourth

Colored Parts	Total Parts	Fraction Colored
1	4	$\frac{1}{4}$

37. Now, fold the paper in half the other way as in the picture below.
Unfold the paper and trace the folds.

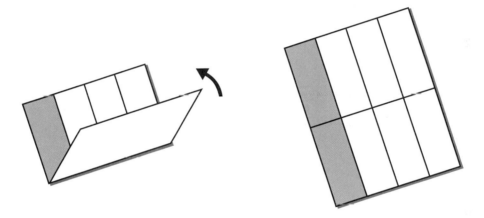

38. Count the colored parts and then count all the parts. Write the
numbers in the first two columns of the table. Then in the last column
write a fraction that is equivalent to one-fourth.

39. Fold the paper as you did in Question 37. Then, fold it again as shown
in the picture below.

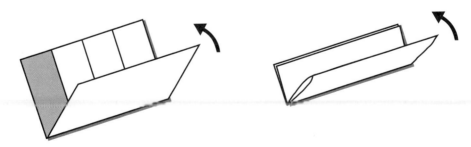

40. How many total parts do you think the paper will have when you unfold it?

41. Unfold the paper and trace the folds. Then, count the colored parts and the total parts. Use your paper to find another fraction that is equivalent to one-fourth. Fill in the third row in the table.

Now, you need to get another sheet of paper.

42. Fold the new sheet of paper in fourths the long way as you did in Question 35. Unfold it and trace the lines between the fourths. Then, color one of the fourths.

43. Fold the paper into thirds the other way as shown in the picture. Then, unfold it and trace the folds.

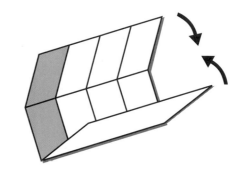

44. Fill in another row in the table.

45. Fold the paper as you did in Question 43. Then, fold it again as shown in the picture below.

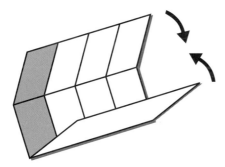
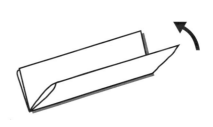

46. How many total parts do you think the paper will have when you unfold it?

47. Unfold the paper and trace the folds. Then, count the parts and fill in another row in the table.

48. The table should now have five rows filled in. What patterns do you notice?

49. Find another fraction equivalent to one-fourth. (Hint: You can write a fraction with 20 in the denominator.)

50. How do you know if a fraction is equivalent to one-fourth?

Unit 18

Viewing and Drawing 3-D

	Student Guide	Discovery Assignment Book	Adventure Book	Unit Resource Guide*
Lesson 1				
Viewing 3-D Objects	@			
Lesson 2				
Drawing 3-D Objects	@	@		
Lesson 3				
Building and Planning Cube Models	@			@
Lesson 4				
Top, Front, and Right Side Views	@			@
Lesson 5				
Problems with Shapes	@			@

Unit Resource Guide pages are from the teacher materials.

Viewing 3-D Objects

A line has only one dimension. You can imagine Mr. Origin sitting on a line. If a bug travels on one-dimensional objects, it can move in only one way with respect to Mr. Origin: left or right. The bug must stay on the line.

1. On a **one-dimensional object,** you can measure length. What units can be used to measure one-dimensional objects?

Left   Right

The objects below have two dimensions. Flat shapes are **two-dimensional (2-D)** objects. If a bug travels on a 2-D object, it can get anywhere it wants to go by moving in two ways: left/right and front/back.

2. On a two-dimensional object, you can measure length and area. What units can be used to measure the area of two-dimensional objects?

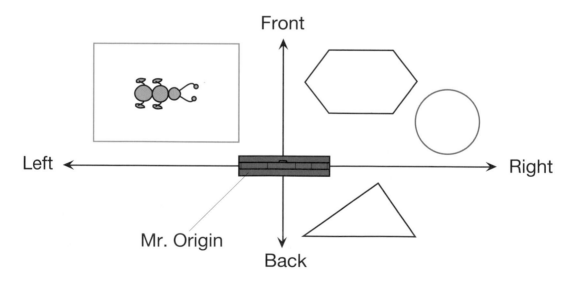

Below is a drawing of an object that has three dimensions. If a bug travels inside a **three-dimensional (3-D)** object, it can get anywhere it wants by moving in three ways: left/right, front/back, and up/down.

On a three-dimensional object, you can measure length, area, and volume. Most things in everyday life have three dimensions.

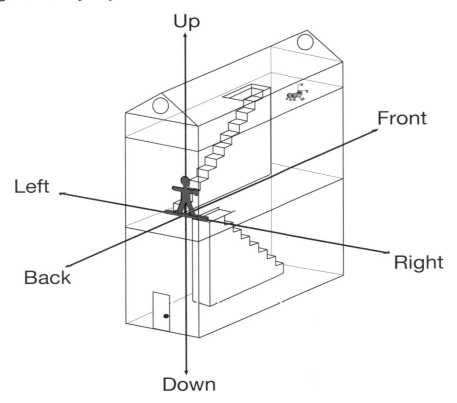

3. What units can be used to measure the volume of 3-D objects?

A tissue box is a 3-D object. It is an example of a **rectangular prism.** Use a tissue box to answer Questions 4–5.

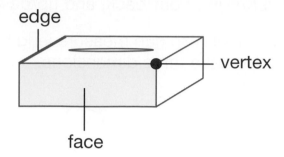

4. **A.** How many faces does your box have?

   B. How many edges does your box have?

   C. A **vertex** is a corner. **Vertices** are corners. How many vertices does your box have?

5. Move the box around in your hands or on your desk to see different views.

   A. What do you have to do to see only one face? Describe what you did in words or show your classmates how to do this.

   B. Move the box around so that you see only two faces. Describe what you did.

   C. Hold the box so that you are looking directly at one vertex. How many faces can you see?

   D. Can you see four faces at once? Five? All six? If you can, describe or show how.

6. The pictures below are drawings of a tissue box. Each shows a different view. How many faces do you see in each drawing?

A.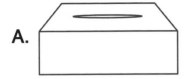

B.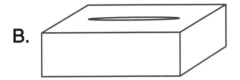

C.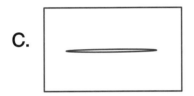

7. Describe how to position yourself and your box so that you can see each of the three views in Question 6.

Drawing 3-D Objects

Drawing a Cube by Showing Three Faces

You can use geometry to help you learn to draw a cube. Studying the edges, faces, and vertices of a cube will help you draw what you see when you look at a cube. A **cube** is a box that has six faces. All the edges of a cube are the same length.

1. Here are 3 sketches of a cube. Which look like a cube? Which do not? Explain your choices.

A. 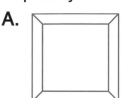 B. 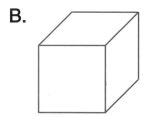 C.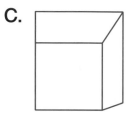

2. Using what you have learned, try to draw a cube.

Use either of these two methods to practice drawing a cube. You can also come up with a method of your own.

Drawing a Cube by Showing Three Faces

3. Draw a square for the front face.

4. Draw three small, parallel lines going back from the top corners and one side corner. These lines must be the same length.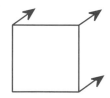

---

5. Draw two connecting lines. The first line should be along the top and the second line should be along the side.

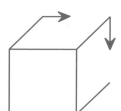

Drawing a Cube by Showing Its Skeleton

6. Draw a square for the front face.

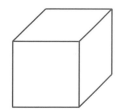

7. Above and to the right of the first square, draw another square of the same size. Notice that one corner of each square is in the center of the other square, forming a new, smaller square.

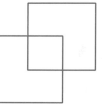

8. Connect the four corners of the first square with the same corners of the second square.

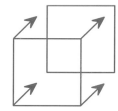

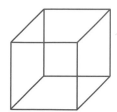

9. How are the drawings from the two methods alike? How are they different?

Extension

You can use toothpicks and small marshmallows to make a 3-D cube model of your own. You will need one toothpick for each cube edge. You will also need 8 marshmallows for the vertices, which you can use to connect the toothpicks.

A. Stick one end of a toothpick into a marshmallow.

B. Make a square corner by sticking another toothpick into the marshmallow.

C. Put marshmallows on the empty ends of the toothpicks. Connect enough toothpicks and marshmallows to make one square face of your cube.

D. Make another square as in step C.

E. Follow the same steps used in the drawing *Showing a Cube's Skeleton* to finish building your toothpick cube.

Now, you have a cube!

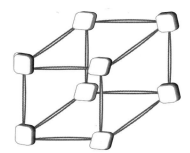

Building and Planning Cube Models

Dee is a toy designer who works for the Cube Toy Company. Her job is to write a booklet that gives children ideas about what they can build with the cubes. She works with the connecting cubes, finds a factory design she likes, and tries various ways to record her design in her booklet.

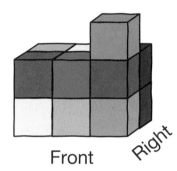

Front   Right

Dee's Drawing of the Factory

First, she provides a two-dimensional drawing of her three-dimensional cube model as shown in her drawing.

Use connecting cubes to build Dee's cube model factory.

Dee also makes a cube model plan for the cube model on a grid. Place your model of the factory on Dee's cube model plan.

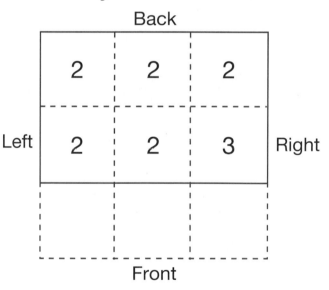

Factory Cube Model Plan

Back

2	2	2
2	2	3

Left   Right

Front

On a sheet of paper on her desk, Dee recorded some measurements.

- Which measurement is the volume of the factory?

- Which measurement is the area of the factory's floor plan?

- Which measurement is the height of the factory?

Factory

3 units

6 square units

13 cubic units

Building and Planning Cube Models

Turn your factory upside down. What shape is the floor of the factory?

The bottom of a model is called its **base,** or **floor plan.** The base is outlined on the cube model plan. Place the bottom of your factory directly on top of the cube model plan again. Be sure the front of the factory is towards the front of the plan.

Dee looked at the building from above to draw the cube model plan. Now, place your factory beside the cube model plan. Look at the numbers written on the plan. What do you think the numbers stand for?

A cube model plan provides lots of information about a cube model. With a cube model plan, you can find the area of a cube model's base, its volume, and its height.

Dee uses rules in making her cube models. Dee's cube model plans only work if we stack cubes in a certain way.

These pictures represent some rules for making cube models. Can you explain them in words? Why do you think we use these rules?

1. Below are cube model plans for four cube models. Build the model for each plan. (The plans are a scale drawing, not actual size.) Then, record the area of its base, its volume, and its height. Remember to use the proper units with each of your answers.

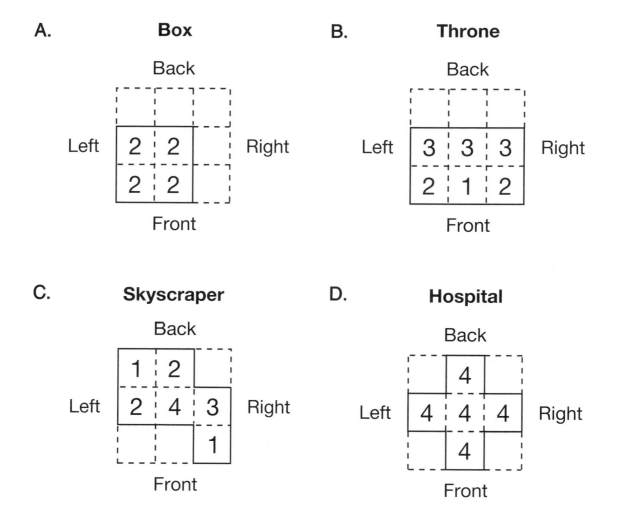

A. **Box**

Back

Left | 2 2 / 2 2 | Right

Front

B. **Throne**

Back

Left | 3 3 3 / 2 1 2 | Right

Front

C. **Skyscraper**

Back

Left | 1 2 / 2 4 3 / 1 | Right

Front

D. **Hospital**

Back

Left | 4 / 4 4 4 / 4 | Right

Front

2. Dee needs to finish her booklet by next week, but she doesn't have enough cube models yet. Help her out by building a model that she can include in her booklet. Follow these guidelines:

- Make sure that the base of your model is no larger than a 3-by-3 square. (That way, you won't have any problems recording it.)

- The volume of your model should not be greater than 27 cubic units.

- Record your cube model in a cube model plan. You can use a copy of the *3 × 3 Cube Model Plans* Activity Page.

- Be sure to give the model you create a name and to write it on the plan.

3. Build the models described in A through F. Then, make a cube model plan for each. (Hint: There may be more than one answer or, sometimes, no solution is possible.)

   A. The floor plan is a 2-by-3 rectangle. The height is 3 units. The volume is 17 cubic units.

   B. The base has an area of 6 square units. The floor plan is not a rectangle. The volume is 24 cubic units.

   C. The floor plan is a 3-by-3 square. The height is 3 units. The volume is 26 cubic units.

   D. The volume is 18 cubic units. The floor plan is a 3-by-3 square. The height is 2 units.

   E. The area of the base is 4 square units. The height is 3 units. The volume is 14 cubic units.

   F. The volume is 30 cubic units. The height is 5 units.

Top, Front, and Right Side Views

Use the cube model plan to make Dee's factory with cubes.

Factory Cube Model Plan

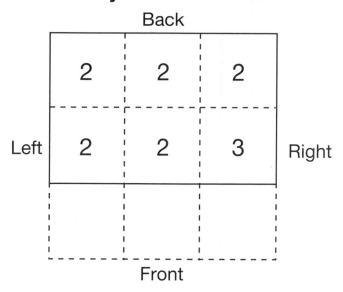

Back

| 2 | 2 | 2 |
| 2 | 2 | 3 |

Left   Right

Front

Factory Top View

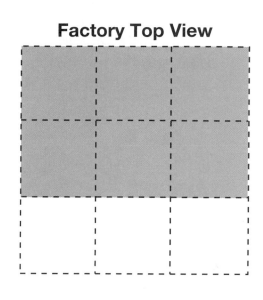

Dee also shows three **views** of her cube models: a **top view,** a **front view,** and a **right side view.** Compare the Factory Top View to the cube model plan.

The top view does not show as much information as the cube model plan. By looking only at the top view, can you tell what the cube model's volume is? What about its height? The shape of its floor plan?

Look at both the front and right sides of your factory model. Compare what you see to the front view and right side view Dee recorded below.

Factory Front View

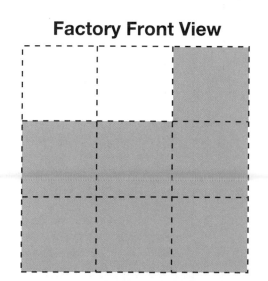

Factory Right Side View

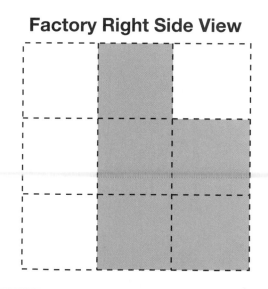

Here is a cube model plan for another model Dee designed.

Dee recorded three views of her "house with garage" model below. Unfortunately, she forgot to label them. Use this cube model plan to build the house with garage. Can you tell which view is the top view? The front view? The right side view?

House with Garage

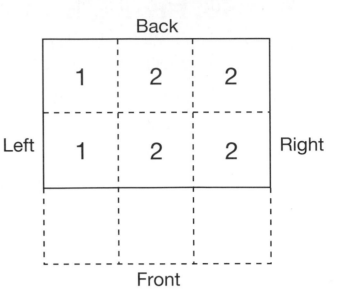

Back

1	2	2
1	2	2

Left ... Right

Front

A

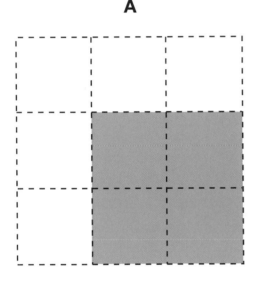

C

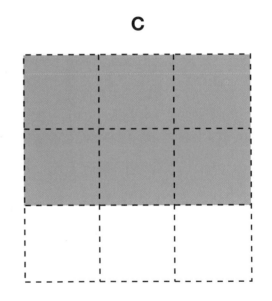

B

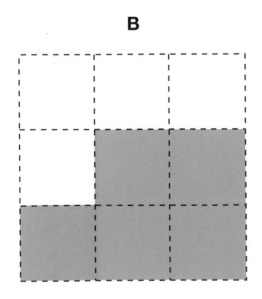

Dee's assistant, Tonya, made a cube model and called it a "hotel." Here are the cube model plan and right side view for the hotel.

Hotel

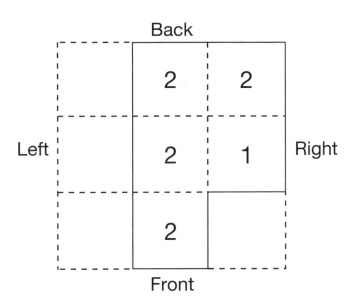

Hotel Right Side View (Tonya)

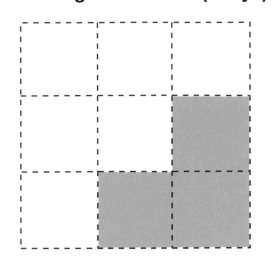

Do you think Tonya's right side view is correct? Why or why not?

Dee built the hotel and told Tonya that she didn't think Tonya's right side view was correct. Dee made the right side view shown here.

Use the cube model plan to build the hotel. Do you think Dee is correct? Why or why not? Place your hotel model on the overhead projector with the right side facing up. (Your teacher can help you.) Which view do you see? Tonya's or Dee's?

Hotel Right Side View (Dee)

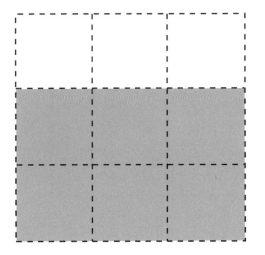

Top, Front, and Right Side Views

Recording Three Views

Build cube models using the cube model plans in Questions 1–4.
(The squares on the plans are a scale drawing, not actual size.)
Record the top, front, and right side views of each cube model on
Three-view Records.

1.

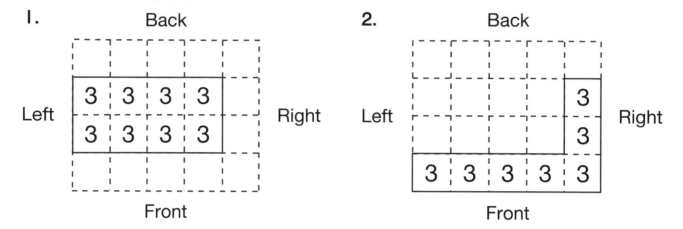

2.

3.

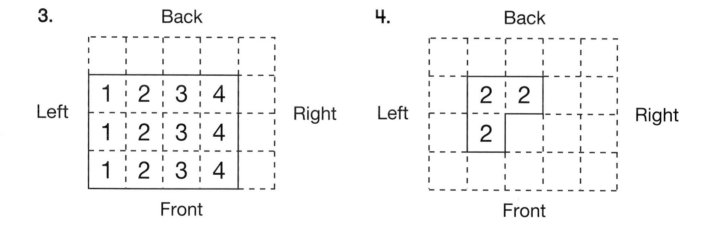

4.

Cube Model Puzzles

Build cube models using the information given in Questions 5–8 below. Then, record your answers on a copy of the *3 × 3 Cube Model Plans* sheet. Some puzzles may have more than one solution.

5.   **Front View**

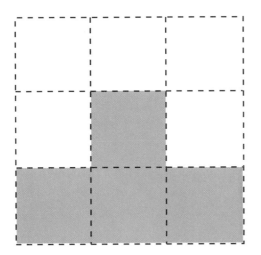

The volume is 6 cubic units.

6.   **Top View**

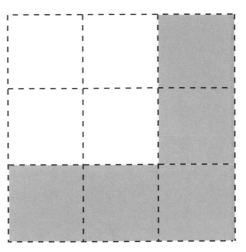

The height is 3 units.
The volume is 15 cubic units.

7.   **Right Side View**

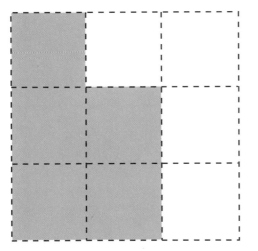

The volume is 12 cubic units.
The floor plan is a 2-by-3 rectangle.

8.   **Top View**

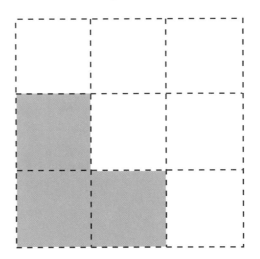

The height is 4 units.
The volume is 11 cubic units.

Problems with Shapes

Cereal Boxes and Tissue Boxes

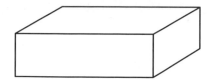

1. Draw a box like this one on your paper.

2. Trace three parallel lines on your drawing in blue.

3. Color one face of your drawing green.

4. Put a red dot on all the vertices you can see in your drawing. How many dots did you make?

Revisit Tiny TIMS Town

Here are the cube model plans for 4 buildings from Tiny TIMS Town:

2	2	2
3	2	2

school

2	2
2	2

bank

3	1
3	

market

4

library

5. Which building has the largest volume?

6. Which building has the smallest volume?

7. What is the area of the base of each building?

8. The market is planning to expand so that the floor plan will look like this:

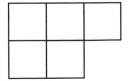

There is a height limit of 4 units in Tiny TIMS Town. The market owners want to double the volume of their store using this floor plan. Draw cube model plans to show two ways they could expand the market.

Unit 19

MULTIPLICATION AND DIVISION PROBLEMS

	Student Guide	Discovery Assignment Book	Adventure Book	Unit Resource Guide*
Lesson 1				
Break-apart Products	◎			
Lesson 2				
More Multiplication Stories	◎			
Lesson 3				
Making Groups				
Lesson 4				
Solving Problems with Division	◎			◎

Unit Resource Guide pages are from the teacher materials.

Break-apart Products

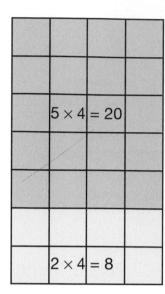

One way to solve a multiplication problem is to break it apart into easier problems.

Example: Find 7×4.

Look at this 7×4 rectangle.

There are $5 \times 4 = 20$ red squares and $2 \times 4 = 8$ green squares.

So, $7 \times 4 = 5 \times 4 + 2 \times 4$

$\qquad = 20 \; + \; 8$

$\qquad = 28$

1. On a separate sheet of grid paper, draw a 7×3 rectangle.

   A. Color the first 5 rows red.

   Complete: $5 \times 3 = ?$

   B. Color the last 2 rows green.

   Complete: $2 \times 3 = ?$

   C. Complete these number sentences for your rectangle.

   $7 \times 3 = ? \times 3 + ? \times 3$

   $7 \times 3 = \quad ? \quad + \; ?$

   $\qquad = \quad ?$

2. Draw a 6 × 8 rectangle on grid paper.

   A. Color the first 5 rows red. How many squares are red? Finish this number sentence: 5 × 8 = ?

   B. Color the last row green. How many squares are green? Write a number sentence for this part.

   C. How much is 6 × 8? Use these number sentences to help you.

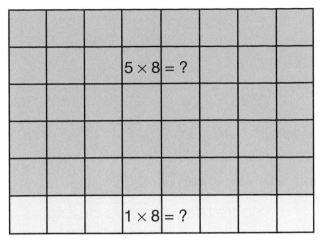

   $6 \times 8 = ? \times 8 + ? \times 8$

   $6 \times 8 = \quad ? \quad + \quad ?$

   $\qquad = \quad ?$

3. Draw a 3 × 8 rectangle horizontally on your grid paper.

   A. Color the top two rows red.

   B. Color the bottom row green.

   C. Complete: $3 \times 8 = ? + ?$

   $\qquad\qquad\quad = ?$

4. Draw rectangles of the following sizes. As in Questions 1–3, break each rectangle into two pieces by coloring. Then, compute the answer using easier products. Write number sentences beside your rectangles to show your answers.

   A. 7 × 8   B. 9 × 6

5. Use rectangles to help solve the following problems. Write number sentences beside your rectangles.

   A. 3 × 12   B. 4 × 15   C. 2 × 17

Break-apart Products   **SG · Grade 3 · Unit 19 · Lesson 1** 287

6. Rachel found 5×12 by breaking the 12 apart. One part was a 10.

$$5 \times 12 = 5 \times 10 + 5 \times 2$$
$$= 50 \quad + \quad 10$$
$$= 60$$

Ben found 5×12 by breaking the 12 into two equal parts:

$$5 \times 12 = 5 \times 6 + 5 \times 6$$
$$= 30 \quad + \quad 30$$
$$= 60$$

Solve the following problems by breaking them apart. Use Rachel's method at least twice, and use Ben's method at least twice.

A. $5 \times 18 = ?$ **B.** $16 \times 3 = ?$

C. $6 \times 14 = ?$ **D.** $4 \times 23 = ?$

E. $13 \times 4 = ?$ **F.** $2 \times 36 = ?$

Homework

You will need *Centimeter Grid Paper* to complete this homework.

Hannah broke apart a rectangle to find 12×4. Her solution is shown below.

There are
$8 \times 4 = 32$
green squares
and $4 \times 4 = 16$
red squares.

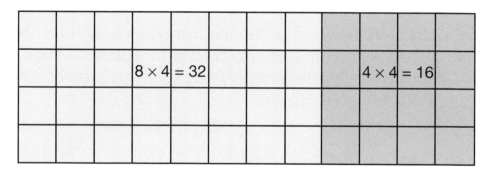

So, $12 \times 4 = 8 \times 4 + 4 \times 4$
$$= 32 \quad + \quad 16$$
$$= 48$$

1. On a separate sheet of *Centimeter Grid Paper* draw a 12×4 rectangle. Use this rectangle to show a different method than Hannah's. Write number sentences beside your rectangle to show your answer.

2. Draw two 14 × 4 rectangles on a sheet of *Centimeter Grid Paper*. Find 14 × 4 by breaking the rectangles apart. Show two different methods. Write number sentences beside your rectangles to show your answers.

Find the following products by breaking them apart into simpler products. Use *Centimeter Grid Paper* to help you.

3. 5 × 12

4. 2 × 15

5. 5 × 24

6. 14 × 3

7. 9 × 6

8. 3 × 13

Review

Find the following products any way you like. You do not have to use the break-apart method. You may use your multiplication table to help you.

9. 10 × 4 = 40

10. 7 × 20

11. 3 × 60 = 180

12. 5 × 70

13. 9 × 30 = 630

14. 8 × 20

15. 4 × 40 = 160

16. 6 × 80

17. 7 × 90

18. 5 × 80

19. 9 × 40

20. 3 × 50

More Multiplication Stories

Students in Mr. Jones's class wrote stories and drew pictures to show how they solved some multiplication problems.

Here is Peter's story for the problem 4×26:

> A farmer had 4 chicken pens. Each held 26 chickens. How many chickens did he have in all?

Here is Peter's solution to the problem 4×26:

> $26 = 25 + 1$. First, I find 4×25. To do that, I double 25 to get 50. I double that and get 100. I know that 4×1 is 4. So, $4 \times 26 = 100 + 4 = 104$.

Peter decided to change his story so that it matched the solution to his problem. Here is his new story and his picture:

> A farmer had 4 pens. Each held 25 brown chickens and 1 red chicken. How many chickens did he have in all?

Peter's Story

```
BBBBBBBBBB        BBBBBBBBBB        BBBBBBBBBB
BBBBBBBBBB        BBBBBBBBBB        BBBBBBBBBB
BBBBB             BBBBB             BBBBB
R                 R                 R
```

```
BBBBBBBBBB
BBBBBBBBBB
BBBBB
R
```

$4 \times 26 = 4 \times 25 + 4 \times 1$

Brown   Red
Chickens   Chickens

Here is Libby's story for the problem 72 × 3.

> 72 children at my brother's preschool have tricycles. How many wheels are on the tricycles?

Here is Libby's solution to the problem 72 × 3:

> 72 = 70 + 2. 70 × 3 is the same as 3 × 7 tens. That's 21 tens, which equal 210. 2 × 3 = 6. So, 72 × 3 = 210 + 6 = 216.

Libby changed her story to match her solution to the problem and drew a picture:

> 70 families in my brother's preschool had tricycles. Then, 2 more children got tricycles for their birthdays. How many wheels are on all the tricycles?

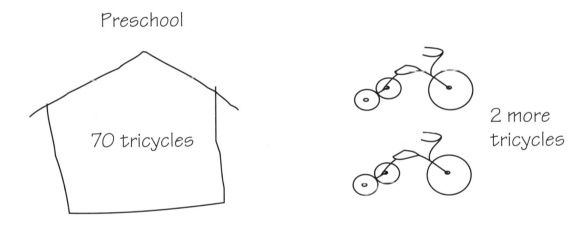

$$72 \times 3 = 70 \times 3 + 2 \times 3$$

wheels on   wheels on

old tricycles   new tricycles

To solve 72 × 3, Libby broke 72 into 7 tens and 2 ones.

Alex solved the problem 63 × 4 by breaking 63 into tens and ones. He used a computer to draw his picture. Notice that Alex's story matches the way he solved the problem. He broke 63 into 60 + 3. He solved 60 × 4 and 3 × 4. Then, he added the pieces.

Problem: 63 × 4

Old horses

60 horses wear   60 × 4 = 240 shoes

New horses

3 horses wear   3 × 4 = 12 shoes

63 horses wear   240 + 12 = 252 shoes ANSWER

Story: There were 60 horses on a farm. The farmer bought 3 more horses. Every horse wore 4 horseshoes. How many shoes did they wear altogether?

Solving Problems Tyrone's Way

Tyrone solved the problem 5 × 37 by breaking 37 into tens and ones. He wrote a story that matches the way he solved it. To organize his work, he wrote the problem at the top of the page and divided the solution into four parts: "Products to Calculate," "Calculations," "Story," and "Picture."

Instead of drawing all those flies, he used tracker shorthand to represent them.

Problem: 5 x 37

<u>Products to Calculate</u>

5 x 30

5 x 7

<u>Calculations</u>

$$5 \times 30 = 150$$
$$5 \times 7 = 35$$
$$5 \times 37 = 150 + 35$$
$$= 185 \text{ ANSWER}$$

<u>Story</u>

There were 5 giant lizards.

Each one ate 37 flies.

First, they ate 30 flies for lunch. Then, they ate 7 more for snacks.

How many did they eat in all?

<u>Picture</u>

Solve the following problems by first breaking the two-digit number into tens and ones and then multiplying. For each problem, write a story, and draw pictures to match your solution. Organize your work the way Tyrone organized his. You may use your multiplication tables to help you with any facts you need.

1. $3 \times 54 = ?$ $= 162$ 2. $31 \times 8 = ?$ $=$
3. $5 \times 67 = ?$ $=$ 4. $45 \times 6 = ?$ $=$
5. $4 \times 28 = ?$ $=$ 6. $62 \times 5 = ?$ $=$
7. $58 \times 5 = ?$ $=$ 8. $7 \times 36 = ?$ $=$

Solving Problems Maria's Way

Maria recorded her work like this:

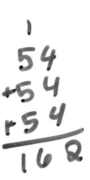

$$
\begin{array}{lll}
37 & \rightarrow & 30 + 7 \quad \text{step 1} \\
\underline{\times 4} & & \\
28 & \leftarrow & 4 \times 7 \quad \text{step 2} \\
\underline{+ 120} & \leftarrow & 4 \times 30 \quad \text{step 3} \\
148 & & \text{answer}
\end{array}
$$

Solve the following problems, showing your work as Maria did.

9. $21 \times 8 = ?$ 10. $84 \times 3 = ?$
11. $75 \times 3 = ?$ 12. $61 \times 5 = ?$
13. $46 \times 8 = ?$ 14. $52 \times 9 = ?$
15. $34 \times 6 = ?$ 16. $91 \times 5 = ?$

Homework

Solve the following problems, showing your work as either Tyrone or Maria did.

1. $2 \times 87 = ?$ 2. $23 \times 9 = ?$ 3. $9 \times 13 = ?$
4. $34 \times 9 = ?$ 5. $4 \times 79 = ?$ 6. $18 \times 7 = ?$
7. $6 \times 68 = ?$ 8. $53 \times 8 = ?$ 9. $42 \times 5 = ?$

10. Solve 3×37. Write a story and draw a picture to match your solution.

More Multiplication Stories

Solving Problems with Division

Story Problems

Solve the following problems. For each problem, explain how you found your solution.

1. We bought 12 packages of juice boxes. Each package had 6 boxes. How many boxes did we buy?

2. Juan bought 200 marbles. Each bag contained 50 marbles. How many bags of marbles did he buy?

3. Juan divided his 200 marbles equally among himself and his four friends. How many marbles did each of them get?

4. For her birthday, Anne wants to invite six friends to go skating with her. If tickets cost $1.50 per person, how much will it cost for Anne and her friends to skate?

5. Each cupcake box holds a half dozen cupcakes. How many boxes are needed to hold 48 cupcakes?

6. Five children found $3.00 on the playground. When no one claimed it, the principal said they could share it equally. How much did each child get?

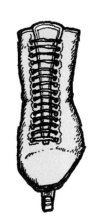

Multiply or Divide?

7. Look back over the problems you solved in Questions 1–6. Write number sentences for each one. Which problems have multiplication sentences and which have division sentences?

Problems with Remainders

Each of the following problems involves division and remainders. For each problem, deal with the remainder in a way that makes sense for the question asked.

8. The 250 children from Johnson Elementary School were going on a field trip. Each bus could hold 60 children. How many buses would they need?

9. Julia earned $1.00 and wanted to spend it to buy some fancy pencils for school. If each pencil costs $.30, how many pencils could she buy?

10. The Johnson Elementary School ordered 21 pizzas for the 4 third-grade classes to share equally. How many pizzas did each class get?

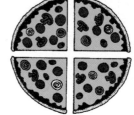

11. The 23 students in a third-grade classroom were divided into four groups. Each group should be as close to the same size as possible. How many students were in each group?

Your Division Stories

12. Write your own stories to match the following division problems. Then, solve the problems. Include in your stories what happens to any remainders.

    A. $26 \div 5 = ?$

    B. $75 \div 10 = ?$

    C. $140 \div 2 = ?$

The Bake Sale

Mrs. Joseph's class is planning a bake sale. Help them plan for it by solving the following problems and explaining how you got your answers. Some solutions might involve both multiplication and division.

13. Kate can make 3 dozen cupcakes for the bake sale. If she puts four cupcakes in each bag, how many bags of cupcakes will she have?

14. The class plans to buy cans of frozen lemonade. Each can makes 64 oz of lemonade. If they buy four cans, how many 6-oz cups can be filled?

15. George is going to make 64 brownies for the bake sale. If he puts 4 brownies in each bag and each bag sells for $.50, how much money will they make selling George's brownies?

16. Tess is going to make 90 crispy treats and divide them equally into 30 bags. The price for one bag of crispy treats is $.75.

    A. How much does one crispy treat cost?

    B. How much will they make if they sell all the crispy treats?

Homework

Solve the following problems.

1. $2 \times 8 = ?$
2. $9/3 = ?$
3. $6 \times 7 = ?$
4. $30 \div 5 = ?$
5. $28/4 = ?$
6. $7 \times 9 = ?$
7. $45 \div 5 = ?$
8. $24/6 = ?$
9. $64/8 = ?$
10. $13/1 = ?$
11. $10/2 = ?$
12. $3 \times 7 = ?$

13. **A.** Elly made one dozen sandwiches for a picnic with 3 of her friends. If the four girls want to share equally, how many sandwiches will each friend get?

    B. Elly's friend Emma brought a 64 oz pitcher of juice to share with the group. How much juice will each friend get?

    C. Elizabeth made 6 cupcakes to share with the group. How many cupcakes will each friend get?

14. Write a story problem to go with one of the multiplication problems in Questions 1–12.

15. Write a story problem to go with one of the division problems in Questions 1–12.

Solving Problems with Division

Unit 20

CONNECTIONS: AN ASSESSMENT UNIT

	Student Guide	Discovery Assignment Book	Adventure Book	Unit Resource Guide*
Lesson 1				
Experiment Review	@			
Lesson 2				
Tower Power		@		
Lesson 3				
Becca's Towers				@
Lesson 4				
Earning Money				@
Lesson 5				
End-of-Year Test				@

Unit Resource Guide pages are from the teacher materials.

Experiment Review

Professor Peabody was working at home redecorating his living room and hall. He used a stencil to make a border around the top of the living room wall. As he worked, he remembered a lab he worked on some months ago.

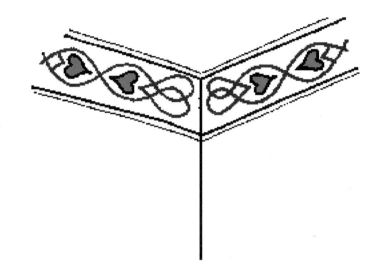

1. Which lab does Professor Peabody remember?

2. Answer the following questions about that lab. You may use earlier units in the *Student Guide* or your portfolio to help you.

   A. What variables did you study in the lab?

   B. Did you have to keep any variables the same so that the experiment would be fair? If so, which ones?

   C. Did you measure anything? If so, what?

   D. How many trials did you do? If you did more than one trial, tell why.

   E. What kind of graph did you make, a point graph or a bar graph?

   F. What were the most important problems you solved using your data and your graph?

3. Look at the picture of Professor Peabody in his lab. This picture and the work in your portfolio can help your class make a list of the labs you completed. For each lab, answer each part of Question 2.

Student Rubric: *Knowing*

In My Best Work in Mathematics:

- I show that I understand the ideas in the problem.

- I show the same mathematical ideas in different ways. I use pictures, tables, graphs, and sentences when they fit the problem.

- I show that I can use tools and rules correctly.

- I show that I can use the mathematical facts that apply to the problem.

Student Rubric: *Solving*

In My Best Work in Mathematics:

- I read the problem carefully, make a good plan for solving it, and then carry out that plan.

- I use tools like graphs, pictures, tables, or number sentences to help me.

- I use ideas I know from somewhere else to help me solve a problem.

- I keep working on the problem until I find a good solution.

- I look back at my solution to see if my answer makes sense.

- I look back at my work to see what more I can learn from solving the problem.

Student Rubric: *Telling*

In My Best Work in Mathematics:

- I show all of the steps that I used to solve the problem. I also tell what each number refers to (such as 15 boys or 6 inches).

- I explain why I solved the problem the way I did so that someone can see why my method makes sense.

- If I use tools like pictures, tables, graphs, or number sentences, I explain how the tools I used fit the problem.

- I use math words and symbols correctly. For example, if I see "6 – 2," I solve the problem "six minus two," not "two minus six."

Index

This index provides page references for the *Student Guide.* Definitions or explanations of key terms can be found on the pages listed in bold.

word problems, 152
and zero, 153

Edge, 268
Equal shares, 90–94
Estimation, 62–64, 213–215
   of sums and differences, 77–78, 80
   mass, 124, 127
   volume, 238
Experiment review, 301

Faces (of a cube), 268
Fact families, multiplication and division, **153**–154
Factor, 145–146, **150**
Facts, turn-around, 146
Fewest Pieces Rule, **47**, 51
Flip, 252
Floor plan (of a cube model), 274
Fractional part of a set, 180–191
Fractions, 480–491
   equivalent, **255**
   with geoboards, 252–254
   with paper folding, 255–263
   and time, 191
   whole-part, 180–182
   word problems, 185–186, 190–191
Front/back axis, **97**–98

Games
   Find the Panda, 101–102
   Fractionland, 188
   Nine, Ten Game, 24–27
   Nothing to It!, 233
   Problem game, 135
   Tens game, 109–110
   Tenths, Tenths, Tenths, 220–221
   Time and Time Again, 201
   Turn Over Game, 7
Geoboard, 252–254

Geometry
   coordinate, 96–108
   dissections, 158–165
   three-dimensional, 266–283
Graduated cylinder, 239
Gram, 115
Graph. *See also* Bar graph, Point graph
   best-fit line, 120–122
   interpreting, 249
   line, 125–127
   patterns on, 83
   predictions using, 84
   straight line, 82–85
Graphing data, 120
Graphs, interpreting, 33

Hexagon, 170
Horizontal axis, **4**, 10, 83

Kilogram, 115

Labs
   The Better "Picker Upper," 60–61
   Fill 'er Up!, 244–248
   Kind of Bean, 8–10
   Length vs. Number, 227–232
   Make Your Own Survey, 203–208
   Mass vs. Number, 119–123
Lab review, 301
Left/right axis, **96**–98
Length
   measuring, 97–100, 106, 108, 273, 275–276
   measuring to the nearest centimeter, 222–226

Line, through data points on a graph, 83
Line symmetry, 169
Linear data, 121, 124–126
Linear function, 249
Liter, 237
Lizardland, 140–144, 152–154

Magic square, 19–21
Mapping
    with coordinates, 97–102, 105–107, 266
    scale, 137, 99–100, 103–108
Mass, 114–119
    estimating, 124, 127
Math facts
    addition, 7, 14–22, 109–110, 233
    multiplication, 32–41, 86–92, 140–155, 286–287
    subtraction, 22–27, 135, 233
Mathhoppers, 86–89
Measurement
    area, 58–61, 136, 169, 171, 273, 275–276, 283
    length, 97–100, 106, 108, 131, 222–226, 273,
        275–276
    mass, 114–117
    volume, 236–249, 273, 275–276, 283
Median, 245
Meniscus, 239
Mental math, 70, 76, 213, 215
Milliliter, 237
Money, 62–64, 93–95, 143, 297
    and decimals, 219–220
    profit, 85
    sales tax, 249
Mr. Origin, 96–98, 266
Multiplication, 32–41, 83–94, 87–92, 137, 142–155,
        151, 286–298
    area model for, 286–289
    array model, 145–148
    break-apart products, 286–294
    by 10s and 100s, 155
    by nine, 149
    fact families, **153**
    fact strategies, 149
    facts, 32–41, 86–92, 140–155, 286–287
    fractions, 40
    number sentences, 36
    rectangles and, 145–148
    stories and pictures, 37–40, 290–294
    word problems, 33–36, 290–294, 297
Multiplication Facts I Know chart, 151

Names, number of letters in, 2–6, 32–33
Number line, jumps on, 86–89
Number sentences, 24–27, 33, 87–89, 92–94, 213, 233,
        246–247
    multiplication, 36

Octagon, 58
One-dimensional, 266
Ordering numbers, 51, 136

Parallel lines, 270–271, 282
Pentagon, 170, 175
Percentage, 202
Perimeter, 166, 169, 171–172
Pictures. *See* Labs
Place value, 44–51
    Fewest Pieces Rule, 47, 51
Point graph. *See also* Labs
    from a bar graph, 83
Populations, 7, **8**
Predictions, 6, 8, 106–107, 246. *See also* Labs
    using data tables, 137
    using graphs, 84, 130
    using linear patterns, 122–125
Prime numbers, 146
Product, 150
Proportional reasoning, 137

Quadrilateral, 170, 175

Rectangle, 58
Rectangular prism, 268
Remainder, 296–298
Right angle, 166, 169, 171–172
Rulers, reading, 223–226

Sample, 7, **8**
  of animals, 9–10
Sampling, 2–6
Scales
  reading, 242
  reading a ruler, 223–224
Sides
  edges, 166–172
  of a polygon, 166
Skip counting, by tenths, 219
Spinners, 16
Spinning Sums game, 16
Square centimeters, 59
Square numbers, 147
Stencils, 130–134
Strategies
  addition facts, 14–16
  subtraction facts, 22–24
  for winning a game, 7
Student Rubric: Knowing, 303
Student Rubric: Solving, 304
Student Rubric: Telling, 305
Subtraction
  with base-ten pieces, 71–73, 211–212
  facts, 22–27, 135, 233
  paper-and-pencil, 73–76, 211–215
Sum, 16
Survey, 2–6, **203**
Symmetry. *See* Line symmetry, Turn symmetry

Tangrams, 158–165
Thermometer, percentage, 202
Three-dimensional, 267
Time, 194–201
  on an analog clock, 196–198, 201
  on a digital clock, 201
  and fractions, 191
  reading clocks, 54–55, 196–198, 201
  word problems, 56, 197–198
TIMS Laboratory Method, 9, 61
Triangle Flash Cards, activities with, 150
Turn symmetry, 172
Turn-around facts, 146, 149
Two-dimensional, 266

Variable, 4, **9.** *See also* Labs
  value, **10**
Vertex, 166, 169, **268**
Vertical axis, 4, 10, 83
Views, top, right, and side, 277–281
Volume, 236
  of cube models, 273, 275–276, 283
  by displacement, 241, 243
  measurement, 236–249
  units, 267

Word problems, 11, 62–64, 90–92, 136–137, 142–144, 148, 176–177, 185–186, 190–191, 197–198, 249, 297. *See also* Labs
  addition, 111
  addition and subtraction, 74–75, 79–80, 213–215
  division, 152, 295–297
  multiplication, 33–36, 41, 290–294
  time, 56

X-axis, 96

Y-axis, 97

Zero, dividing by, 153